COOKIES

Natalie Hartanov Haughton

HPBooks
a division of
PRICE STERN SLOAN
Los Angeles

Natalie Hartanov Haughton

Natalie Haughton's culinary interest developed at an early age. Her mother, an excellent cook and baker, always welcomed and encouraged her in the kitchen. Some of Natalie's earliest and fondest childhood memories include helping with the baking of special cookies at Christmas time. Natalie's fascination with food led her to pursue a food-oriented career.

Natalie graduated from the University of California with a Home Economics degree. Since that time, her career has included working for an advertising agency and major food companies in public relations, consumer education, recipe development and food photography. Currently, she is food editor for the Daily News, Los Angeles. Natalie shares her creative recipe and writing talents with readers on a weekly basis, offering food information and articles on the local, national and international scene.

Natalie, her husband Fred and their two children, Alexis and Grant, reside in Studio City, California. The family is adventuresome in sampling experimental foods whenever the occasion arises and enjoys specialty cookie-making projects.

Published by HPBooks
a division of Price Stern Sloan, Inc.
11150 Olympic Boulevard
Suite 650
Los Angeles, California 90064

Cover photography by Anthony Nex, Los Angeles
Cover food styling by Carole Reece
Interior Photography by deGennaro Studios, Los Angeles
Interior food styling by Carol Flood Peterson

ISBN 0-89586-254-9
Library of Congress Catalog Card Number 83-81729
© 1983 Price Stern Sloan, Inc.
Printed in the U.S.A.
12 11 10 9 8 7 6

This book has been printed on acid-free paper.

Cover photo: Medley of Cookies

Contents

Cookie Basics

Cookies have universal appeal. They are one of the most basic sweets—a delightful treat year in and year out. Cookies are plain fun. Who doesn't look forward to the aroma of freshly baked cookies drifting through the kitchen, warm cookies fresh from the oven or a cookie jar filled with home-baked creations?

Connoisseurs have their favorite specialties. Some like their cookies crisp and chewy, others like them soft and moist and still others prefer them buttery rich and sweet. Cookies come frosted or unfrosted, big or small and in countless shapes, textures and flavors.

The number of cookie variations is mind-boggling. There are cookies for every occasion from snacks and picnics to the most elegant party.

Generally, cookies are made from basic ingredients—butter, sugar, flour, eggs, liquid and leavening in varying proportions. Flavors are added by using spices, fruits, nuts, extracts, chocolate and cereals.

Cookies are the trademark of many skilled bakers. Their creations add a special touch to the cookie jar, lunch box, holiday cookie tray or any-occasion gift box.

Although the origin of the cookie seems to be lost in history, the name comes from the Dutch word *koekje,* meaning *little cake.*

Mention of cookies can be found in America's first original cookbook, *American Cookery,* published in 1796. Author and cook Amelia Simmons described the preparation of a cookie with a stiff dough containing butter, sugar, sour cream and flour, seasoned with ground coriander.

For most, cookies bring back treasured childhood memories—a nostalgic taste of days gone by. Whether it's mom's toffee squares, auntie's molasses cookies or grandpa's fruit bars, no doubt there's one cookie you remember fondly that stands head and shoulders above the rest.

While cookies rank high in popularity throughout the year, they come into their own during the holidays. In many homes, holidays and homemade cookies are synonymous—a cherished tradition.

How well I remember our holiday baking sessions when I was a child. We couldn't wait to help mom with cookie-making activities—a little delicious nibbling was allowed here and there. Certain cookies with special flavors, shapes and decorations were made only during this festive season. They represented the art of cookie baking at its highest. Although some were time-consuming, they were well worth waiting for.

More cookies are baked at holiday time than at any other time of year. Not only to serve family and friends, but to share as gifts with relatives, friends, bosses, teachers and that special someone in your life.

Cookie specialties span the world. Italy has its Pizzelles; Norway, Berlinerkranser; Denmark, Butter Cookies; Scotland, Shortbread; Greece, Kourambiedes; Scandinavia, Krumkakes and Rosettes; France, Macaroons; and Germany, Pfeffernüsse, Lebkuchen and Springerle. And the United States has everyone's favorite, the Original Toll House ® Cookie.

Whether you're searching for familiar favorites or looking for something unique to add to your cookie repertoire, explore the collection here. Some are plain, others fancy. Some are quick and easy to make, others complicated and time-consuming. Each has its own special flavor and appeal. Besides tasting incredibly good, these cookies are geared to suit nearly every occasion and preference.

With one-bowl mixing—by hand or electric mixer—these updated recipes cut time and effort to a minimum. Yet goodness is kept at a maximum.

Let's face it—there's nothing quite like homemade cookies. Try one of these recipes and enjoy some today. Happy cookie baking!

Kinds of Cookies

Cookies come in an endless number of varieties, sizes, shapes and flavors. There are six types of cookies categorized by the way the dough is shaped: bar, drop, refrigerator, molded, pressed and rolled.

Bar Cookies are the easiest to make because the soft dough is spread in a baking pan. Once baked, they are cut into squares, bars or triangles. All the dough is baked at once, making bar cookies a real timesaver. You can store or tote them in the baking pan in which they've been baked. Make bar cookies if your time is limited.

Drop Cookies are made by dropping soft dough into mounds on baking sheets, generally two inches apart. Follow directions for spacing in each recipe. Use a small rubber spatula or another spoon to assist in pushing the dough off the spoon. Some cooks, including youngsters, find it easier to use a finger as a pusher. Some also use a cookie dropper, a special kitchen gadget made for dropping cookie dough. This is probably the easiest cookie to make next to bar cookies, although more time is consumed in several bakings.

Refrigerator Cookies involve a two-step procedure—preparation and baking—which occur at different times. First, prepare and shape the dough, usually into a log or roll. Then, wrap and refrigerate the dough several hours, a day or up to a week. Most of these doughs can also be frozen six to eight weeks. Cookies are sliced and baked at another time. Be sure the dough is well wrapped to prevent drying out in the refrigerator or freezer. A double thickness of waxed paper, foil or plastic wrap works well. Twist the ends and seal with tape or place the roll in a plastic bag and seal. Refrigerator cookie dough is great to have handy to bake on a moment's notice when unexpected guests drop by.

Molded Cookies are made by forming firm dough into desired shapes such as balls, crescents, wreaths or pretzels. Sometimes it may be necessary to chill the rich dough for easier handling. Children enjoy helping in molding tasks, providing it is simply a matter of rolling the dough into balls. Mother may find that chore easy, but time-consuming, particularly if the recipe makes a large quantity.

Pressed Cookies are made by forcing dough through a cookie press or pastry bag. This gives an array of designs shaped by the template or decorating tube used. Pressed cookies are usually more time-consuming and complicated than other types of cookies.

Rolled Cookies use a stiff dough that is rolled out on a lightly floured surface or baking sheet. Then the dough is cut into shapes using cookie cutters, a knife and pattern, a pastry wheel or specially designed wooden molds or rolling pins. Usually the dough is chilled before rolling. If the chilled dough becomes too stiff and difficult to roll, allow it to stand at room temperature until pliable. Children enjoy lending a helping hand with cookie cutting and decorating.

Successful Cookie Baking

Here are a few general hints that will help ensure success with your cookie baking.

Read through the recipe. Check to see that all ingredients and equipment are on hand. Use the finest quality fresh ingredients available. Follow ingredient amounts and directions the first time around. Once you are familiar with the recipe, vary spices and personalize it to suit your needs and tastes. Keep in mind that a slight change in the proportions of major ingredients can change the result dramatically.

Allow butter or margarine to come to room temperature, if the recipe requires. Measure ingredients accurately so dough is the proper consistency. Use liquid-measuring cups for liquids and graduated measuring cups for dry ingredients. Rounded or heaping measurements may affect results.

Preheat oven 10 to 15 minutes before baking. Oven temperature is extremely important. Check it with an oven thermometer. Don't be like the upset, frustrated lady who tried numerous times, but was unable to duplicate her friend's cookie recipe. It turned out her oven was 50F (25C) off. And all the time she thought it was her baking skills!

Use the one-bowl mixing method for the majority of these recipes. Sifting together flour, leavening and spices prior to adding to the butter-sugar mixture is really a matter of personal preference.

Doughs can be mixed quickly with an electric mixer. Follow the recipe directions which include creaming together butter or margarine, sugar, egg, if used, and flavoring on medium speed. Then beat in flour, leavening and spices at low speed until blended. Turn mixer to medium speed and continue beating until well blended, being careful not to overmix. Most cookies can also be mixed by hand, using a wooden spoon, but more effort is required.

Some cookies require an electric mixer. These include Madeleines, Ladyfingers, Macaroons and Basic Almond-Paste Cookie Dough.

Use vegetable shortening to grease baking sheets and pans when recipe indicates. In a few instances, butter is suggested. Strive to make all cookies in the same batch the same size, shape and thickness. Distribute them evenly and neatly on baking sheets. Bake cookies, one sheet at a time, in the center of the oven. This will give best results and even browning. If baking two sheets at a time is necessary, switch and rotate sheets halfway through baking time.

Baking times are based on baking one sheet at a time, unless otherwise noted. To avoid overbaking, check cookies for doneness three to four minutes before recipe indicates. Use a timer to avoid guessing. Remember ovens vary and overbaked cookies are a disappointment. A few minutes can make a big difference. When baking several batches of cookies, let baking sheets cool between bakings. A hot sheet can change the character and shape of the cookies.

Once baked, immediately remove cookies to racks to cool completely, unless recipe directs differently. Otherwise, cookies will continue to cook. Allow cookies to cool in a single layer. Fragile or delicate cookies are often cooled on baking sheets a few minutes before removing to racks to cool completely. This helps to minimize breakage. If cookies have cooled too long on the sheets and are difficult to remove, place them in the oven briefly to soften; then remove from the sheet. In general, cool cookies completely before storing, frosting and decorating or cutting into bars or squares. Follow directions with each recipe.

Frost cookies with homemade or commercially prepared frostings. Decorate with colored sugar and sprinkles, chocolate shot, silver dragées or assorted candies. Use a pastry bag fitted with assorted decorating tubes to pipe on frosting.

These hints should start you on your way to successful cookie baking. Well, what are you waiting for—get baking!

6

Cookie-Cutting Guide

Cut bar cookies into a variety of sizes and shapes. The size of the bar or square is approximate and will vary with your pans.

8-INCH-SQUARE BAKING PAN

Number of Rows	Size of Bar	Yield
4 x 4	2" x 2"	16
4 x 5	2" x 1-1/2"	20
4 x 8	2" x 1"	32
5 x 5	1-1/2" x 1-1/2"	25
6 x 6	1-1/4" x 1-1/4"	36

NOTE: A 9-inch-square baking pan will yield the same number of cookies as above, but each cookie will be a little larger.

11" x 7" BAKING PAN

Number of Rows (Length x Width)	Size of Bar	Yield
5 x 4	2-1/4" x 1-3/4"	20
5 x 5	2-1/4" x 1-3/8"	25
8 x 4	1-1/2" x 1-3/4"	32
8 x 5	1-1/2" x 1-3/8"	40
11 x 4	1" x 1-3/4"	44

13" x 9" BAKING PAN

Number of Rows (Length x Width)	Size of Bar	Yield
6 x 6	2-1/8" x 1-1/2"	36
8 x 5	1-5/8" x 1-3/4"	40
8 x 6	1-5/8" x 1-1/2"	48
6 x 9	2" x 1"	54

15" x 10" JELLY-ROLL PAN

Number of Rows (Length x Width)	Size of Bar	Yield
10 x 4	1-1/2" x 2-1/2"	40
12 x 4	1-1/4" x 2-1/2"	48
8 x 6	1-3/4" x 1-3/4"	48
10 x 5	1-1/2" x 2"	50
9 x 6	1-5/8" x 1-5/8"	54
10 x 6	1-1/2" x 1-1/2"	60

How to Cut Diamonds and Triangles

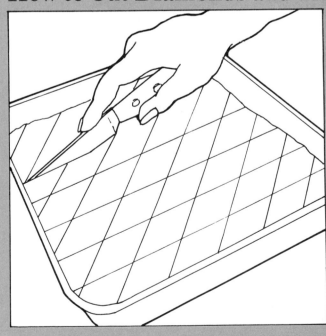
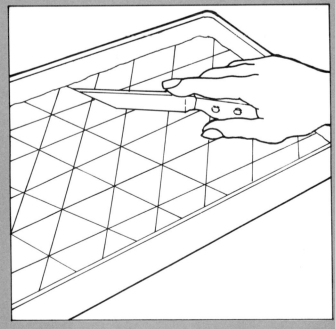

For easy use, trace these cookie patterns and use for Circus Animals & Party Animals Carousels recipe, page 144.

Cookie Ingredients

To achieve the best results when baking cookies, here are a few tips on ingredients.

Butter or Margarine—There is no substitute for the rich flavor butter gives to cookies. Butter contains salt, therefore many of the recipes calling for butter require a minimum of salt. Unsalted or sweet butter is occasionally used where a special delicate flavor is desired. Regular butter can be substituted in the recipe providing the quantity of salt, if any is called for, is decreased. Use unsalted butter in making clarified butter.

Butter and margarine are used interchangeably in many recipes; however, be aware that a richer flavor is obtained when using butter. Unless you must use margarine for economic or health reasons, butter is recommended. Margarine is not a calorie saver—both butter and margarine contain about 100 calories per tablespoon.

Butter or margarine refers, in all cases, to the stick type, not the whipped, tub or diet style. Do not attempt to substitute other fats.

Other Fats—Use hydrogenated vegetable shortening when a recipe calls for shortening. This is suggested for greasing baking sheets unless the recipe states butter. Lard is used in Chinese Almond Cookies for a more tender, flaky result. When a recipe calls for oil, use vegetable oil.

Flour—In a recipe calling for all-purpose flour, either bleached or unbleached all-purpose flour can be used. All flour is unsifted unless otherwise noted. Measuring flour correctly is important. It can mean the difference between a fabulous, tender cookie and a tough, dry one. To measure flour, spoon straight from the bag into a graduated dry-ingredient measuring cup. Level with the straight edge of a knife.

Some of the recipes use whole-wheat flour. Generally, do not substitute whole-wheat flour for all-purpose flour. Results will not be the same. In many cases the end result will be a dense, heavy, dry cookie with a nutty flavor. If you want to experiment, start by substituting whole-wheat flour for no more than half the all-purpose-flour measurement.

Whole-wheat pastry flour is milled finer than regular whole-wheat flour. Using it results in finer textured cookies.

Use cake flour, made of soft wheats, only when specifically designated. Cake flour yields a more tender, lighter cookie. Use cake flour for best results in delicate cookies such as Ladyfingers and Kourambiedes.

Rice flour, available in oriental-food stores and the oriental-food section of supermarkets, is used in some shortbread to yield a more tender product.

Do not use self-rising flour. It requires adjustments in the leavening ingredient in the recipe.

Eggs—Eggs bind ingredients together and are often the only liquid in a cookie recipe. Using the correct size is important. Recipes in this book were tested using large eggs. Substituting different size eggs may affect the texture and consistency of the dough and finished cookie.

Take eggs directly from the refrigerator and separate when cold. For greatest volume, allow egg whites to come to room temperature before beating. When beating egg whites, be sure to use a glass or stainless bowl and beaters that are free of grease. Store leftover egg whites in the refrigerator. Use within a couple of days or freeze for use at a future date. Thaw before using. Egg yolks can be covered with water and stored in the refrigerator two to three days. Drain off water before using. Or, mix with a few pinches of salt or sugar, package and freeze. Thaw before using.

Sugar—Use the type of sugar called for in the recipe—granulated, brown or powdered sugar. Use light-brown sugar unless dark is designated. Pack brown sugar firmly in a dry-ingredient measuring cup. When the word *sugar* stands alone in a recipe it means granulated sugar. Besides adding sweetness and tenderness to doughs, sugar helps in the browning process.

Do not attempt to substitute honey for sugar in a recipe. Look for recipes specifically designed to use honey.

Baking Powder—As a leavening agent, baking powder on an ingredient list refers to double-acting baking powder. Check the expiration date on the package prior to using. Measure baking powder carefully to avoid upsetting the balance of ingredients in the recipe. Cookies collapse when too much baking powder is used.

Baking Soda—This is a neutralizing and

leavening agent. Baking soda is added to dough when acids such as molasses, honey, spices, buttermilk, lemon juice, cream of tartar or fruits are present. Sometimes a recipe calls for both baking soda and baking powder. In such cases, the baking soda usually neutralizes the acid in the recipe while the baking powder is responsible for the main leavening action.

Sweetened Condensed Milk—Condensed milk contains 40 to 45% sugar and 28% milk solids. The balance is water. Keep refrigerated after opening. Do not substitute evaporated milk for sweetened condensed milk—they are not the same. Evaporated milk does not contain sugar.

Whipping Cream—Heavy cream or whipping cream contains 30 to 36% milkfat.

Chocolate—Recipes call for unsweetened or baking chocolate, semisweet chocolate, unsweetened cocoa and chocolate-coating wafers. White chocolate, although not really chocolate, is also used.

To melt chocolate, place in the top of a double boiler. Heat over hot but not boiling water until melted and smooth, stirring occasionally. Avoid having water come in contact with the melting chocolate. It will cause chocolate to seize up and stiffen. Melting chocolate over direct heat is not recommended. It scorches easily.

You can also melt chocolate, uncovered, in a glass measuring cup or custard cup in a microwave oven. Be sure to watch it carefully. Figure on one to two minutes, depending on the amount of chocolate, but check progress closely. The chocolate will retain its shape and may not look melted. When the appearance changes from dull to shiny, this is the signal to stir the chocolate until smooth.

In a recipe calling for cocoa, use unsweetened cocoa. If you want to substitute cocoa for chocolate, use 3 tablespoons unsweetened cocoa and 1 tablespoon shortening (butter, margarine or oil) for each ounce of unsweetened chocolate. Results will not be as rich and velvety.

Chocolate-coating wafers, available at candy- or cake-decorating-supply stores, are ideal for melting. This chocolate remains shiny when spread on cookies like a frosting.

Rolled Oats—Use regular or quick-cooking oats, uncooked, in recipes calling for rolled oats, unless a specific type is designated.

Cereals—Cereals enhance cookies by adding a variety of flavors and textures. When granola is specified in a recipe, it refers to 100% natural cereal made from a blend of rolled oats, whole wheat, coconut and almonds, sweetened with brown sugar and honey. Grape-Nuts is one of the best cereals for adding crunchiness.

Food Coloring—Use liquid or paste colors. Liquid colorings are readily available in supermarkets. Paste colors are sold at cake-decorating-supply stores. Add liquid coloring, one drop at a time, until desired shade is obtained. Paste colors are much more concentrated than liquid colorings. They yield deeper, more vivid colors, so use sparingly. Add paste colors on the tip of a wooden pick to the mixture being colored.

Flavorings—Use pure extract rather than imitation for best flavor.

Spices—Use fresh spices for best results. Store spices tightly closed in a cool dry place. If you have room, store in the refrigerator or freezer to retard deterioration.

Nuts—Nuts add interesting flavor and texture to cookies. Purchase nuts when the crop is fresh, generally in the late fall or around holiday time. Sample your purchases immediately and return any that are rancid.

Store shelled nuts in the refrigerator up to six months. Freeze for longer storage. To blanch nuts with warm skins, such as almonds, submerge in boiling water 1 minute. The warm skins will pop off easily when you squeeze them with your fingers. Toasting nuts releases the natural oil and enhances their flavor. To toast nuts, spread on a baking sheet. Bake in a preheated 325F to 350F (165C to 175C) oven 10 to 15 minutes. Check often to avoid overbrowning.

Nuts are quickly chopped or ground to a fine powder in the food processor with a few quick on/off turns. Watch carefully so you don't end up with nut butter. If you are planning to do a great deal of cookie baking, chop one or two bowlfuls and keep on hand for future use.

When buying nuts, a pound of shelled walnuts or pecans is equal to about four cups.

Cookie Equipment & Storage

STANDARD EQUIPMENT

Baking Sheets & Pans—Shiny heavy-gauge aluminum baking sheets with low or no sides are recommended. Sheets should be two inches shorter and narrower than the oven. Avoid dark baking sheets because they absorb heat and may cause overbrowning on the bottoms of cookies. Non-stick baking sheets and pans work well, providing the non-stick finish is not too dark-colored. Grease baking sheets only when specified. Otherwise, cookies may spread too much.

Place cookie dough on cold baking sheets to avoid undesirable spreading and misshapen cookies. When baking several batches of cookies, wait for the baking sheet to cool between bakings. Or, place the dough on foil and slide the baking sheet under the foil. Bake immediately. Arrange unbaked cookies evenly on baking sheets, generally two inches apart, unless recipe specifies otherwise.

Sometimes it is desirable to line baking sheets or pans with foil to ensure easy removal of baked cookies. Foil is also a time-saver at busy baking times when you need the same pan for more than one kind of cookie. Bar cookies can often be removed in one piece with foil intact and the pan cleaned and reused immediately.

Working with more than one baking sheet will save time, particularly if the recipe makes a large quantity. I found a 17" x 14" baking sheet the most practical size.

When making bar cookies, use the size pan specified in the recipe. Bar cookies are most often baked in an 8- or 9-inch-square baking pan, 13" x 9" baking pan, 11" x 7" baking pan or 15" x 10" jelly-roll pan. For the Fairy-Tale Gingerbread House, you'll need at least one 18" x 12" sheet-cake pan, available in many cookware shops.

If it is necessary to substitute a different pan for the size called for in the recipe, calculate the surface area of the pan by multiplying the pan's dimensions. Then substitute another pan with a similar surface area. For example, two 11" x 7" baking pans with a combined total surface area of 154 square inches could be substituted for a 15" x 10" jelly-roll pan with a surface of 150 square inches. It may be necessary to make minor adjustments in the baking time.

Cooling Racks—Most cookies should be removed with a wide spatula to wire cooling racks immediately after baking. Do not stack warm cookies as they may stick together. If cookies become too cool, you may have difficulty removing them from the pan. If so, return them to the oven one to two minutes to soften; then remove cookies. Cooling racks are available in a variety of shapes. If you do a lot of cookie baking, you may want to invest in several racks. Be sure to elevate racks which don't have legs to allow for sufficient air circulation.

Double Boiler—A double boiler is used for melting chocolate and chocolate mixtures. If you don't have a double boiler, create one by setting a heatproof bowl in a saucepan. Make sure the bowl rests on the edge of the pan above the water, not down in it.

Food Processor—Cookie dough can be prepared in a food processor using a steel blade. Be sure the volume of dough is not too large for your processor bowl. The dough will process in seconds rather than minutes as in an electric mixer. Stir in items such as nuts, shredded vegetables, fruit or coconut at the end of processing, otherwise they may become overprocessed.

Rolling Pin, Pastry Cloth & Sleeve—A rolling pin is a necessity for preparing rolled cookies. If you plan to prepare many rolled cookies, a pastry cloth and stockinette rolling-pin sleeve are wise investments. They prevent sticking and make rolling tasks easier and less messy. To use, sprinkle the heavy woven-cotton cloth generously with flour. Roll the sleeve-covered rolling pin over it to distribute the flour on both materials. After each use, scrape off any dough and shake off excess flour.

Pastry Bags & Decorating Tubes—Some cookies require a pastry bag and round or open-star decorating tube for shaping and decorating. You'll be amazed at the professional-looking results you obtain. The best bags are pliable and plastic-coated inside. They are easy to use and clean. Parchment-paper bags can also be used.

Decorating bags come in sizes ranging from 8 to 14 inches long. Washable bags can be used several times. Use large 12- to 14-inch bags when using large plain round or star decorating tubes. Select the decorating tube to suit desired usage. It may be necessary to trim the bag so the metal decorating tube will fit. Do so carefully. When using a pastry bag and smaller decorating tubes, use a coupler. This allows for easy changing of the tubes while decorating.

SPECIALTY COOKIE EQUIPMENT

Although the equipment listed below is not a necessity, you may enjoy having some of it for cookie-making fun. Many specialty cookies require molds, irons, cookie cutters or cookie presses.

Pizzelle Cookie Iron—Electric and non-electric models are available for making these large thin round, traditionally anise-flavored, Italian cookies with a pretty pattern.

Krumkake Iron—This special iron is used for making Scandinavian cookie rounds that are most often rolled into cones while warm. They can be eaten plain or filled.

Madeleine Mold—A special mold used for making little shell-shaped French cake-like cookies, reminiscent of sponge cake.

Rosette Iron—A long-handled iron which comes with a variety of design forms for making delicate fried cookies.

Springerle Rolling Pin or Wooden Molds—Both can be used for preparing the classic German anise-flavored cookies known as *Springerle*.

Miniature Individual Tart Pans—One- to three-inch-diameter miniature fluted tart pans are available. They are excellent for preparing cookie-like tarts.

Cookie Press or Gun—A press is necessary for making spritz or pressed cookies. They are available with assorted design templates.

Stoneware Shortbread Molds—When baking shortbread, use these molds for a decorative design.

Cookie Cutters—A variety of shapes, sizes and styles are sold. Start a collection of your favorites. Animals, numerals, cartoon characters and a wide array of designs are available.

Artist's Brushes—Brushes of various sizes are needed for decorating with frosting paint.

Fattigmand Roller/Cutter—Use this special roller for making "poor man's" cookies quickly.

Rolling Cookie Cutter—Roll this cast aluminum cylinder marked with assorted designs across rolled-out cookie dough to cut cookie patterns. None of the dough goes to waste.

STORAGE

Prior to storing, cool baked cookies completely. Cookies are best stored in a cool place. Store crisp and soft cookies separately.

Crisp cookies are best stored in a jar or container with a loose-fitting lid. If cookies soften during storage, recrisp them by spreading them on a baking sheet and heating three to five minutes in a preheated 300F (150C) oven.

Soft cookies should be stored in a tightly covered container. If cookies have a tendency to dry out, add a piece of bread or an apple slice to the container to keep cookies moist and maintain softness. Replace apple often.

Bar cookies are best stored covered with foil or plastic wrap in the original baking pan.

Cookies are best eaten fresh, but they can be stored in the freezer up to two months. After that, they begin to lose flavor and quality.

To freeze, cool cookies completely before wrapping in moisture- and vapor-proof paper or freezer containers. You can quick-freeze or flash-freeze cookies before wrapping for freezer storage, if desired. Place the cookies, uncovered, on a tray in the freezer. Freeze until solid. Remove, wrap airtight, label, date and return to freezer.

It's best to frost and decorate cookies after freezing and thawing. Frozen cookies will thaw unwrapped in about 10 minutes at room temperature. If desired, freshen them by heating at 300F (150C) five to seven minutes.

Unbaked dough can also be frozen, properly wrapped, six to eight weeks.

Cookie Gifts & Parties

COOKIE GIFTS FROM YOUR KITCHEN

A most appreciated gift is something from the kitchen. Personalized cookie gifts to relatives, friends, neighbors and business associates are joyous ways to show your warm remembrance.

A treat, created with love as well as of time and talent, is often the most thoughtful present. It will work wonders to get you in the spirit of the occasion. Consider the unlimited number of delicious cookie creations you can make. No doubt your culinary repertoire is already bulging with favorite recipes.

Cookies need not be time-consuming or complicated to prepare. Many can be made on short notice. Make sure they are scrumptious and wrapped with festive flair. If you are a newcomer to the cookies-from-your-kitchen routine, start out by making several batches of one or two cookies. This limits the confusion and number of different ingredients, as well as shopping and baking steps. Limiting variety will save time and trouble.

Cookie gifts are doubly special when cleverly packaged and presented. Half the fun is searching for the perfect container that fits the budget, suits the particular goodie and will be kept long beyond the last marvelous nibble.

Container ideas abound in cookware shops, housewares departments, import stores, drug stores, supermarkets and card shops. Pick up baskets, pottery or glass containers or jars, cookie jars, wooden boards, old-fashioned tins or decorative plates.

Imagination, ingenuity and creativity are the keys to unique packaging. Be continually alert for new ideas. When you least expect, you will find a perfect packaging idea.

Label the cookies attractively with serving and storing instructions. Then they will be enjoyed at peak quality and flavor. Using pretty labels printed with your name gives a professional look. Tuck in the recipe, if desired.

When it comes to wrapping, the sky's the limit. Here's a chance for your creativity to shine. Brightly colored bags, plastic wrap, colored cellophane, fabric trimmed with lace and colorful ribbons will do the trick. Interesting tie-ons such as cookie cutters, wooden spoons, special ornaments for the Christmas tree, mini copper molds, mini whisks, spatulas, a pastry brush, a zester, spices or aluminum scoops all add to the whimsy.

Use coffee or shortening cans wrapped with attractive gift wrap and decorated as desired for cookie-gift containers. You can paint them or decorate with self-adhesive paper. Have the children design and color wrapping paper.

Another time, line an attractive basket with a colorful potholder, kitchen towel or a piece of pinked fabric and add a selection of cookies. Cookies can be packed in pretty cannisters, in a large ceramic bowl, on a pretty serving plate, in plastic storage containers, in a metal pail, in a soufflé dish or fancy mold or on a wooden board.

Decorated egg cartons with their individual slots make wonderful containers for an assortment of cookies. First, fill with tinted grass or colored tissue. Then pile cookies on top. Decorate the egg carton with paper cutouts, stickers or whatever strikes your fancy. Kids will love helping. Attach a large bow before giving.

Flower pots, brightly painted and decorated, along with matching saucers make interesting containers. Select the appropriate size to suit the quantity of cookies you are giving. Spray paint and decorate several pots at once. Then keep them handy for spur-of-the moment cookie gifts.

At Easter time, fill grass-stuffed baskets with an assortment of egg- and bunny-shape cookies. A 9-inch-tall hollow chocolate egg filled with assorted cookies and confections makes a gorgeous gift or edible centerpiece. Nestle it in a colorful basket tied with a bow. Decorate the egg with tinted frosting flowers and write *Happy Easter* with white coating chocolate.

Lattice strawberry or cherry-tomato baskets from the supermarket produce section make economical cookie containers. Weave basket with ribbon and tie on a bow. Filled with cookies, they are attractive but inexpensive.

For a novel wrap, let the children draw a cute face on a paper plate. Then attach it to a cellophane-encased cookie tin, complete with a twisted ribbon for the hair.

You can give your package a theme, if desired. Give shortbread with a shortbread mold, Pizzelles with a pizzelle iron, festive-shaped and decorated cutout cookies with cookie cutters or bars in an appropriate size pan.

What a nice way to wrap up gifting—with a batch of cookies! Wouldn't you cherish receiving a delicious creation from a loving-cook's kitchen?

PACKING & MAILING COOKIES

A package of homemade goodies mailed to loved ones far away is always a special treat. Wherever the cookies are headed, here are some packing and shipping guidelines.

For mailing and shipping, choose unfrosted cookies that are sturdy and keep well. When selecting recipes, consider the humidity, hot and cold temperatures and rough handling the package may encounter. Bars, fruit cookies, drop and molded cookies are the best travelers.

Check with your local postmaster or shipper with regard to shipping times and deadlines. This is especially important during the holiday rush. Add a couple of days to the delivery timetable to ensure arrival in time for a holiday or special occasion. Also, double check on any special packaging and wrapping requirements.

Proper wrapping is essential. Package cookies in layers in waxed-paper- or foil-lined tins or unbreakable containers with tight-fitting lids. Baskets, cardboard and plastic boxes, or coffee and vegetable-shortening cans with plastic lids work well. Place a cone, point side up, on the bottom of the can. This acts as a cushion for cookies. To make the cone, cut a paper circle 1/2 inch larger in diameter than the base of the can.

Make a cut in one place from edge to center of the paper circle. Overlap to make a cone shape; tape to secure. Place in the bottom of the can. The point of the cone should extend about 1/2 inch off the floor of the can. Place cookies in can around cone, filling snugly almost to the top. Check to make sure the lid will fit. Pad the top with a little crumpled waxed paper. If sending more than one kind of cookie, place the heaviest kind on the bottom. Better yet, wrap different cookies separately to avoid blending flavors.

If the cone idea doesn't appeal to you, wrap cookies in groups of four or six, depending on size, in a single layer of foil or plastic sandwich bags, sealing or tying securely.

Keep the outer wrapping of the can or container simple. Elaborate decorations traveling across the miles rarely last long enough to impress. Cover the container in bright paper, gaily printed fabric or paint with bright lacquer colors. Trim with colored ribbon or attractive stickers.

Set the gift container in a strong corrugated carton or packing box, padding well with styrofoam pellets or chips, crumpled or shredded newspaper or plastic bubble-wrap for cushion.

Nylon strapping tape and clear or brown sealing tape are recommended for sealing packages. Do not use masking or plastic tape as it will not secure the package well. If mailing the package, do not use string or twine over the outer package as it will catch in postal processing machinery.

After the final wrapping, place the "ship to" and "return" address on one side of the package. Place transparent tape over the address to protect it from weather and possible blurring. You may also mark the package *perishable*, *fragile* or *handle with care*, although this is no guarantee of gentle handling. Also include both addresses inside the package as a safety precaution in case the package is torn open or the address becomes unreadable.

Remember, no matter how securely the cookies are wrapped, the condition of the goodies at the final destination depends on the weather, handling, temperature and many factors beyond the sender's control.

COOKIE PARTIES

No holiday season would be complete without traditional cookie-baking. And what better way to get in the holiday spirit than with a fun and festive cookie party. Adults will enjoy a holiday cookie exchange. Children will love a cookie-making party. Although most popular during the Christmas holidays, a child's cookie-creating party could be staged for any occasion during the year.

CHILDREN'S COOKIE PARTY

Good Times for Cookie Monsters in Your House—If you have young ones at home, start a tradition by turning your kitchen into a busy fragrant Christmas workshop. Invite a number of your children's friends to a holiday cookie-making party. It will be an event they'll long remember. All ages love to pat, roll and decorate cookies.

Organize activities with the age group in mind. Be sure to have plenty of dough ingredients as well as pre-mixed chilled dough on hand. Older children may enjoy preparing and rolling their own dough, but 5- to 8-year-olds will appreciate having dough pre-mixed, chilled and rolled out ready for cutting. Supply each child with a sheet of waxed paper for a handy work surface.

Set out an array of cookie cutters, rolling pins and a bowl containing a mixture of equal parts flour and powdered sugar. This mixture is for dipping the cutters into. If appropriate, give a quick cookie-cutting demonstration before turning the children loose to busy themselves. Have a few baking sheets ready for cutout cookies. Adults are needed to help transfer cookies to baking sheets and to supervise actual baking details.

You may want to have a number of cookies already baked so there won't be a delay in decorating activities. This is especially important for the very young who have limited attention spans. Mom can do this a few days in advance.

Assemble and set out an assortment of frostings, colored sugars, sprinkles, silver dragées, candies, nuts, miniature marshmallows, semisweet chocolate pieces and raisins to allow for creativity in decorating. Be sure to have plenty of cookies for nibbling along the way.

Allow each child to take home several of his creative masterpieces to share with his family.

COOKIE EXCHANGE PARTY

An Idea for the Holidays or Anytime of Year—The holidays are a time for exchanging greetings. Because food plays a key role in the festivities, why not exchange culinary "gifts" with friends and neighbors? Plan to host a cookie exchange and recipe swap.

An exchange is a marvelous way to plan an informal get-together. It also helps solve the problem of many hours in the kitchen baking cookies. You'll end up with a variety of cookies on hand for parties and spur-of-the-moment snacks.

With your home as the trading-post, each participant has an opportunity to bake a favorite cookie to exchange with others. Participants also take home a variety of cookie specialties.

Here's how the party works. Each participant brings enough cookies to trade and sample during the gathering. The hostess should establish the number of cookies to bring prior to sending out invitations. This depends on the number of persons expected to attend. It's a good idea while making the guest list to take a verbal poll to determine the expected response.

Whatever you decide, plan the party well in advance. Mail invitations early so guests can save the date and have sufficient time to bake. Note on the invitation the number of wrapped packages of six cookies each, as well as the number of cookies to be brought attractively arranged on a serving plate for sampling and tasting.

To RSVP, request that guests mail you their cookie recipes two weeks in advance with no exceptions. This allows the hostess time to compile and print sets of recipes to hand out at the party.

While all of this may sound complicated, it's really not. The sample invitation here, based on 10 guests, will serve as a guideline. It shows how easily the party is done.

Some people on your guest list may think the number of cookies is high, but when making one favorite cookie recipe, only a few batches will be needed. By pooling efforts in the exchange, a great deal of baking can be completed.

On the day of the exchange, offer guests coffee, tea and punch. You might even serve some finger sandwiches to balance the high sugar content of the cookies. Be sure to set aside enough room for trays of cookies for sampling.

Identify each contributor's cookies with a printed sign such as "Suzie Jones' Toffee Squares."

To avoid confusion, assign several friends to help sort the packages of wrapped cookies as they arrive. Use large grocery bags or shopping bags marked with each participant's name. When the party is over, guests pick up their bags filled with cookies. It's always fun to see how creatively guests wrap their cookies. Use paper plates or bowls, foil-covered cardboard, baskets, ribbons and colored cellophane to get in the festive mood.

Cookie-Party Sample Invitation

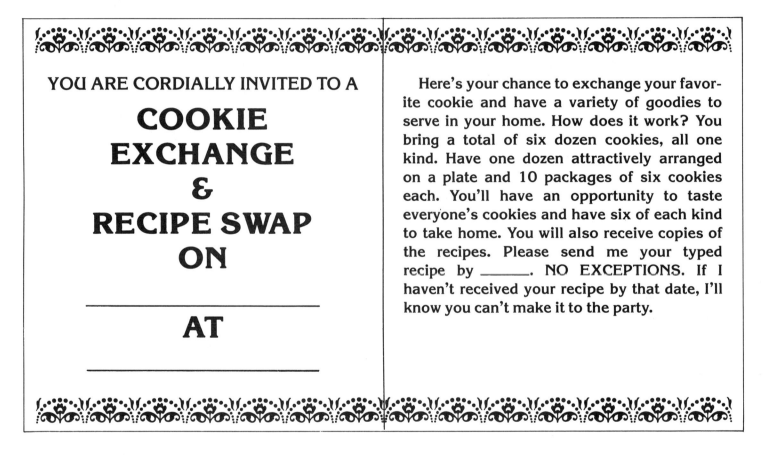

YOU ARE CORDIALLY INVITED TO A

COOKIE EXCHANGE & RECIPE SWAP ON

_____

AT

_____

Here's your chance to exchange your favorite cookie and have a variety of goodies to serve in your home. How does it work? You bring a total of six dozen cookies, all one kind. Have one dozen attractively arranged on a plate and 10 packages of six cookies each. You'll have an opportunity to taste everyone's cookies and have six of each kind to take home. You will also receive copies of the recipes. Please send me your typed recipe by _____. NO EXCEPTIONS. If I haven't received your recipe by that date, I'll know you can't make it to the party.

Add your own date, time and place to the cookie-exchange invitation. Then photocopy onto colored paper. Or, take to a copy business for duplication.

Bar Cookies

Rely on bar cookies when time is at a premium. The easiest of all cookies to make, bars are baked in assorted sizes of square and rectangular pans. Some bars are plain, others are fancy. This collection includes the simple and complex, suited for a variety of occasions.

Bar cookies are ideal to serve at casual get-togethers, picnics and meetings as well as the most elegant, formal parties and teas. Most are great totables, too. Some require refrigeration. Some are so easy that children will enjoy making them for after-school snacks.

When making bar cookies, you'll find lining pans with foil helpful. It keeps the pan clean, aids in easy removal of bars and keeps them from sticking. To line a pan with foil, invert the pan. Tear off foil longer than the pan. Place foil over inverted pan, pressing it to conform to the pan shape. Remove foil; turn pan right-side up. Place shaped foil piece in the pan, pressing into place carefully to avoid tearing.

Custom-cut your bars according to when and how you plan to serve them. For a special tea, a holiday gift tray or a morning coffee break, cut bar cookies into small delicate-size pieces. For lunch boxes or occasions when one special bar will stand alone, large pieces may be in order. The choice is yours. Use the sizes indicated in the recipes as a guide.

Sometimes it is difficult to judge when a bar cookie is done. Watch carefully to avoid overbaking. Remember, baking times are only guidelines because ovens vary. Instinct and common sense are often the best judges of doneness.

When making bars, use the pan size suggested or one nearly the same. If you use a smaller pan, you may end up with cake-like cookies while a larger pan may yield dry, crumbly cookies.

Perhaps you're wondering where to start in this irresistible bar collection. Toffee Squares are old-timers and score high marks as an all-time versatile favorite. If fruited bars tickle your fancy, Old-World Raspberry-Cheese Bars, Apricot-Nut Ribbons and Applesauce-Filled Oat Bars should be appealing.

Go straight to your kitchen and try some of these delicious bar cookies. Your family and friends will praise your tasty treasures.

Old-World Raspberry-Cheese Bars

Cheddar cheese in the crust and topping gives these jam-filled squares a lift.

1-1/2 cups all-purpose flour	1/2 cup butter or margarine
1 teaspoon baking powder	1 cup shredded Cheddar cheese (4 oz.)
Pinch of salt	1 cup raspberry jam
3 tablespoons packed brown sugar	1/2 cup finely chopped walnuts or almonds

Preheat oven to 350F (175C). In a medium bowl, combine flour, baking powder, salt and brown sugar. Using a fork or pastry blender, cut in butter or margarine until mixture resembles coarse crumbs. Stir in cheese. Remove 3/4 cup mixture; set aside. Press remaining mixture evenly in bottom of an ungreased 8-inch-square baking pan. Spread jam evenly over crust. Sprinkle with nuts. Sprinkle with reserved crumb mixture, pressing in gently. Bake 25 minutes or until golden. Cool in pan. Cut cooled cookies into bars. Store in refrigerator. Makes 32 (2" x 1") cookies.

Apricot-Nut Ribbons

Luscious apricot filling nestled between a sugar-cookie-style crust and topped with nuts.

Apricot Filling, see below	3/4 cup chopped almonds or walnuts
3/4 cup packed brown sugar	1 egg
2 cups all-purpose flour	1 teaspoon vanilla extract
3/4 cup butter or margarine	

Apricot Filling:

1 (6-oz.) pkg. dried apricots	1/3 cup sugar
1-1/4 cups water	1 tablespoon lemon juice

Prepare Apricot Filling; set aside. Preheat oven to 350F (175C). Grease a 13" x 9" baking pan. In a medium bowl, combine brown sugar and flour. Using a fork or pastry blender, cut in butter or margarine until size of peas. Remove 1 cup crumb mixture. Stir nuts into 1 cup crumb mixture; set aside. To remaining crumb mixture, add egg and vanilla. Beat until blended and mixture holds together. Press mixture evenly in bottom of greased baking pan. Bake 10 minutes. Spread baked crust evenly with Apricot Filling. Sprinkle with reserved crumb mixture, pressing into filling. Bake 20 minutes or until golden brown. Cool in pan. Cut cooled cookies into bars. Makes 40 (1-3/4" x 1-1/2") cookies.

Apricot Filling:
In a medium saucepan, combine apricots, water and sugar. Bring to a boil, stirring occasionally. Reduce heat to medium. Cover and simmer 15 to 25 minutes until apricots are tender and mixture resembles puree, stirring occasionally. Stir in lemon juice.

Variation
Cranberry-Orange Ribbons: Substitute Cranberry-Orange Filling for Apricot Filling. To make Cranberry-Orange Filling, in a medium saucepan, combine 3 cups fresh or frozen cranberries, 2/3 cup sugar and 3/4 cup orange juice. Bring to a boil. Reduce heat and cook until all cranberry skins pop, about 5 minutes, stirring occasionally. Stir in 2 teaspoons grated orange peel and 2 tablespoons cornstarch mixed with 1/4 cup cold orange juice. Cook until mixture becomes clear, boils and thickens, stirring constantly. Cool. Proceed as directed above. Store baked cookies in refrigerator. Use within 2 to 3 days.

Cream-Cheese Brownies

Dress up brownies with a marbling of sweetened cream cheese.

Cream-Cheese Filling, see below
1/4 cup butter or margarine
1 cup (6 oz.) semisweet chocolate pieces
1/2 cup sugar
2 eggs
2 tablespoons hot water

1 teaspoon vanilla extract
3/4 cup all-purpose flour
1/4 teaspoon baking soda
Pinch of salt
1/2 cup coarsely chopped walnuts, if desired

Cream-Cheese Filling:
1 (8-oz.) pkg. cream cheese,
   room temperature
1/2 cup sugar

1 egg
1 teaspoon vanilla extract

Prepare Cream-Cheese Filling; set aside. Preheat oven to 350F (175C). Grease an 8- or 9-inch-square baking pan. In a medium saucepan, combine butter or margarine and chocolate pieces. Heat over low heat until melted and smooth, stirring constantly. Remove from heat. Stir in sugar, eggs, water and vanilla until combined. Add flour, baking soda and salt, stirring well. Stir in walnuts, if desired. Spread half the chocolate batter evenly in greased baking pan. Top with Cream-Cheese Filling, spreading evenly. Drop spoonfuls of remaining chocolate batter evenly on top of cheese filling, spreading as evenly as possible with a knife. Swirl knife gently through batter to marble. Bake 30 to 35 minutes. Do not overbake. Brownies should be moist in center. Cool in pan. Cut cooled brownies into squares. Store in refrigerator. Makes 25 (1-1/2-inch) brownies.

Cream-Cheese Filling:
In a small bowl, beat cream cheese, sugar, egg and vanilla until smooth.

Peanut-Butter & Chocolate Brownies

Two favorite flavors team up in separate layers in these bars. Great served partially frozen.

1 cup crunchy or smooth peanut butter
1-3/4 cups sugar
3 eggs
1/2 cup butter or margarine,
   room temperature

1 teaspoon vanilla extract
1/4 cup unsweetened cocoa
1/2 cup all-purpose flour

Preheat oven to 350F (175C). Grease an 8- or 9-inch-square baking pan. In a small bowl, blend together peanut butter, 3/4 cup sugar and 1 egg. Press mixture evenly in bottom of greased baking pan. In a medium bowl, beat together butter or margarine, remaining 1 cup sugar, remaining 2 eggs and vanilla until light and fluffy. Add cocoa and flour, beating until thoroughly blended. Spread evenly over peanut-butter mixture in pan. Bake 35 to 40 minutes. Do not overbake. Cool in pan. Cut cooled brownies into bars. Makes about 20 (2" x 1-1/2") brownies.

Tip

Reduce oven temperature by 25F (15C) if a glass baking dish is substituted for a metal baking pan.

Date-Nut Delights

Use pie-crust mix to prepare a quick oat-coconut crust.

Date-Nut Filling, see below
1 (11-oz.) pkg. pie-crust mix
2/3 cup packed brown sugar

3/4 cup rolled oats
3/4 cup flaked or shredded coconut
3 tablespoons orange juice

Date-Nut Filling:
1-1/2 cups chopped pitted dates
1 cup orange juice

1-1/2 tablespoons grated orange peel
1 cup chopped walnuts

Prepare Date-Nut Filling; set aside. Preheat oven to 350F (175C). Grease a 13" x 9" baking pan. In a large bowl, combine pie-crust mix, brown sugar, oats and coconut. Using a fork or pastry blender, blend in orange juice until mixture resembles coarse crumbs. Reserve 1-1/2 cups oat mixture for topping. Press remaining oat mixture evenly in bottom of greased baking pan. Spread Date-Nut Filling evenly over crust. Sprinkle reserved oat mixture evenly over filling, pressing in lightly. Bake 30 to 35 minutes or until golden brown. Cool in pan. Cut cooled cookies into bars. Makes 36 (2-1/8" x 1-1/2") cookies.

Date-Nut Filling:
In a medium saucepan, combine dates and orange juice. Bring to a boil over medium heat, stirring occasionally. Reduce heat and simmer 5 to 8 minutes or until thickened, stirring occasionally. Remove from heat. Stir in orange peel and walnuts.

Variation

Mincemeat-Nut Delights: Substitute Mincemeat Filling for Date-Nut Filling. To make Mincemeat Filling, in a medium bowl, combine 2 cups prepared mincemeat and 1 cup chopped walnuts. Proceed as directed above.

Cheesecake Treasures

Store these tasty cheesecake bites in the refrigerator.

1/2 cup butter or margarine,
   room temperature
1/2 cup packed brown sugar
1-1/4 cups all-purpose flour
1 (8-oz.) pkg. cream cheese,
   room temperature

1/4 cup granulated sugar
1 egg
2 tablespoons milk
2 teaspoons grated lemon peel
1 tablespoon fresh lemon juice
1/2 teaspoon vanilla extract

Preheat oven to 350F (175C). Lightly grease an 8-inch-square baking pan. In a medium bowl, beat together butter or margarine and brown sugar until creamy. Add flour, blending until mixture resembles fine crumbs. Remove 1 cup crumb mixture; set aside. Press remaining crumb mixture evenly in bottom of greased baking pan, building up sides slightly. Bake 12 to 15 minutes or until edges are light golden. Meanwhile, in a medium bowl, beat together cream cheese and granulated sugar until smooth. Add egg, milk, lemon peel, lemon juice and vanilla, beating until blended. Spread cream-cheese mixture evenly over hot baked crust. Sprinkle reserved crumb mixture evenly over cream-cheese mixture. Bake 25 to 30 minutes or until set. Cool in pan. Cut cooled cookies into squares. Store in refrigerator. Makes 25 (1-1/2-inch) cookies.

How to Make Two-Way Almond Bars

1/Score surface of 1 dough rectangle into 4 rows of 8. Press a pecan half in center of each scored bar.

2/Cut remaining rectangle into 32 pieces. Top center of each plain piece with a dollop of melted chocolate.

Two-Way Almond Bars

Two different-looking almond cookies from a single pan.

1 cup butter or margarine, room temperature
2/3 cup sugar
2 eggs
1 tablespoon vanilla extract
1 (7-oz.) pkg. almond paste,
   room temperature, cut into pieces

2 cups all-purpose flour
32 pecan halves
2 tablespoons apricot jam or preserves,
   heated, strained
1/3 cup (2 oz.) semisweet chocolate pieces,
   melted

Preheat oven to 325F (165C). Line a 15'' x 10'' jelly-roll pan with foil. In a large bowl, beat together butter or margarine and sugar until light and fluffy. Add eggs, vanilla and almond paste, beating until well blended. Beat in flour until well blended. Spread mixture evenly in foil-lined pan. Lightly score surface of dough in half so you have 2 rectangles, each measuring 10'' x 7-1/2''. Score surface of 1 dough rectangle into 4 rows of 8, pressing a pecan half in center of each scored bar. Leave other half of dough as is. Bake 25 to 30 minutes or until edges are lightly browned. Cool in pan. Brush pecan-topped cookies with warm jam or preserves. When glaze has set, cut through score lines making 32 pieces with pecan half in center of each. Cut remaining rectangle into 32 pieces. Top center of each plain piece with a dollop of melted chocolate. Let stand until set. Makes 64 (1-3/4'' x 1-1/4'') cookies.

Peanut Bars

Peanuts give crunch to these delicious three-layer bars.

Crust, see below
1 (14-oz.) can sweetened condensed milk
2 tablespoons butter or margarine
2 teaspoons vanilla extract

1 cup chopped dry-roasted peanuts
3/4 cup (4-1/2 oz.) semisweet chocolate
  pieces

Crust:
1/3 cup butter or margarine,
  room temperature
1/3 cup packed brown sugar

1/2 teaspoon vanilla extract
1 cup all-purpose flour

Preheat oven to 350F (175C). Grease an 8- or 9-inch-square baking pan. Prepare Crust. Press crust mixture evenly in bottom and halfway up sides of greased baking pan. Bake 12 to 15 minutes or until edges are golden. In a medium saucepan, combine sweetened condensed milk, butter or margarine and vanilla. Cook over low heat until butter melts and mixture boils and thickens, stirring occasionally. Stir in 1/2 cup peanuts. Spread evenly over baked crust. Bake 15 minutes or until set. Sprinkle with chocolate pieces. Let stand a few minutes until chocolate melts. Spread chocolate evenly over top. Sprinkle with remaining 1/2 cup peanuts. Cool in pan. Cut cooled cookies into bars. Makes 32 (2'' x 1'') cookies.

Crust:
In a medium bowl, beat together butter or margarine, brown sugar and vanilla until creamy. Add flour, beating until blended.

Coconut-Walnut Bars

Made-to-order for coconut fans.

1/2 cup butter or margarine, room temperature
1/2 cup packed brown sugar

1 cup all-purpose flour
Nutty Coconut Topping, see below

Nutty Coconut Topping:
4 eggs
1-3/4 cups packed brown sugar
2 teaspoons vanilla extract
1/4 cup all-purpose flour

2 teaspoons baking powder
1/4 teaspoon salt
2 cups flaked or shredded coconut
2 cups coarsely chopped walnuts or pecans

Preheat oven to 350F (175C). In a medium bowl, beat together butter or margarine and brown sugar until creamy. Beat in flour, blending thoroughly. Press mixture evenly in bottom of an ungreased 13'' x 9'' baking pan. Bake 10 minutes. Meanwhile, prepare Nutty Coconut Topping. Carefully spread Nutty Coconut Topping evenly over hot crust. Bake 25 to 30 minutes or until golden brown. Cool in pan. While warm, cut into bars. Makes 36 (2-1/8'' x 1-1/2'') cookies.

Nutty Coconut Topping:
In a medium bowl, combine eggs, brown sugar and vanilla. Add flour, baking powder and salt, blending well. Stir in coconut and nuts.

Chocolate-Chip Cheesecake Fantasies

If you like cheesecake, orange and chocolate, you'll find these irresistible.

1-1/2 cups graham-cracker crumbs
2 tablespoons sugar
1/3 cup butter or margarine, melted
1 (8-oz.) pkg. cream cheese,
   room temperature
1/3 cup sugar

1 egg
1 teaspoon vanilla extract
1 tablespoon grated orange peel
1 cup chopped walnuts or almonds
1 cup (6 oz.) semisweet chocolate pieces
2/3 cup flaked or shredded coconut

Preheat oven to 350F (175C). In a medium bowl, combine graham-cracker crumbs, 2 tablespoons sugar and melted butter or margarine. Press mixture evenly in bottom of an ungreased 13" x 9" baking pan. Bake 7 to 8 minutes. In a medium bowl, beat together cream cheese, 1/3 cup sugar, egg, vanilla and orange peel until well blended. Spread evenly over baked crust. In a small bowl, combine nuts, chocolate pieces and coconut. Sprinkle evenly over cream-cheese mixture, pressing in lightly. Bake 25 to 30 minutes or until golden brown. Cool in pan. Cut cooled cookies into squares. Store in refrigerator. Makes 48 (1-1/2-inch) cookies.

Frosted Ginger Bars

A subtle coffee glaze accents these spicy cake-like molasses bars.

1/4 cup butter or margarine,
   room temperature
1/4 cup vegetable shortening
1/2 cup packed dark-brown sugar
1 egg
1/2 cup molasses
1/3 cup water
1 teaspoon instant-coffee powder
1 teaspoon vanilla extract

2 cups all-purpose flour
1 teaspoon baking soda
1/4 teaspoon salt
1-1/4 teaspoons ground ginger
1-1/4 teaspoons ground cinnamon
1 cup chopped raisins
3/4 cup chopped walnuts
Coffee Glaze, see below

Coffee Glaze:
1-1/2 cups powdered sugar
1/2 teaspoon instant-coffee powder
1-1/2 tablespoons butter or margarine,
   melted

1/4 teaspoon vanilla extract
2 to 3 tablespoons hot water

Preheat oven to 350F (175C). Grease a 13" x 9" baking pan. In a large bowl, beat together butter or margarine, shortening, brown sugar and egg until light and fluffy. Beat in molasses, water, coffee powder and vanilla. Add flour, baking soda, salt, ginger and cinnamon, beating until blended. Stir in raisins and walnuts. Spread mixture evenly in greased baking pan. Bake 25 minutes or until light golden brown. Do not overbake or bars will be dry. Cool in pan. Prepare Coffee Glaze. While warm, frost top evenly with Coffee Glaze. When glaze has set, cut cooled cookies into bars. Makes 40 (1-3/4" x 1-1/2") cookies.

Coffee Glaze:
In a small bowl, combine powdered sugar, coffee powder, melted butter or margarine, vanilla and enough hot water to make glaze a thin spreading consistency.

Fruited Holiday Bars

A simple but delicious holiday treat with a hint of orange in the glaze.

1 cup butter or margarine, room temperature
1 cup packed brown sugar
2 teaspoons vanilla extract
1/2 teaspoon salt
2 cups all-purpose flour
1/2 cup chopped candied pineapple

1/2 cup chopped red and green
  candied cherries
1 cup raisins or chopped pitted dates
1 cup chopped walnuts
Glaze, see below

Glaze:
1 tablespoon butter or margarine,
  room temperature
1/2 cup powdered sugar

1 tablespoon orange-flavor liqueur or
  orange juice
1 teaspoon water

Preheat oven to 350F (175C). Lightly grease a 13" x 9" baking pan. In a large bowl, beat together butter or margarine, brown sugar, vanilla and salt until light and fluffy. Add flour, beating until blended. Stir in candied pineapple, candied cherries, raisins or dates and walnuts. Spread mixture evenly in greased baking pan. Bake 25 to 30 minutes or until golden. Do not overbake; surface should be slightly soft. Cool in pan. Meanwhile, prepare Glaze. While warm, drizzle Glaze over top. Let stand until set. Cut cooled cookies into bars. Makes about 40 (1-3/4" x 1-1/2") cookies.

Glaze:
In a small bowl, combine butter or margarine, powdered sugar, liqueur or orange juice and water until smooth.

Pineapple-Ambrosia Bars

Filled moist bar cookies, tangy with crushed pineapple.

1 (20-oz.) can juice-pack crushed
  pineapple
1/4 cup granulated sugar
3 tablespoons apricot jam
3 tablespoons cornstarch
1-1/2 cups all-purpose flour
1/2 teaspoon baking soda

Pinch of salt
1-1/2 cups rolled oats
3/4 cup packed brown sugar
3/4 cup vegetable shortening
1/2 cup flaked or shredded coconut
3/4 cup chopped unblanched almonds

Preheat oven to 375F (190C). In a medium saucepan, combine undrained pineapple, granulated sugar, jam and cornstarch. Cook over medium heat until mixture boils and thickens, stirring constantly; set aside. In a large bowl, combine flour, baking soda, salt, oats and brown sugar. Using a fork or pastry blender, cut in shortening until mixture is crumbly. Remove 1-3/4 cups crumb mixture. Stir coconut and almonds into 1-3/4 cups crumb mixture; set aside. Press remaining crumb mixture in bottom of an ungreased 13" x 9" baking pan. Cover with pineapple mixture. Sprinkle evenly with remaining crumb mixture, pressing in gently. Bake 35 to 40 minutes or until lightly browned. Cool in pan. Cut cooled cookies into bars. Store in refrigerator. Makes 40 (1-3/4" x 1-1/2") cookies.

Applesauce-Filled Oat Bars

Applesauce, raisins and nuts nestled between oat-mixture layers for a nutritious coffee-break treat.

**2/3 cup butter or margarine,
 room temperature**
3/4 cup packed brown sugar
1-1/2 cups all-purpose flour
1/2 teaspoon baking soda
1/4 teaspoon salt

1-1/2 teaspoons ground cinnamon
1-3/4 cups rolled oats
1-1/4 cups unsweetened applesauce
3/4 cup raisins or chopped pitted dates
2/3 cup chopped walnuts

Preheat oven to 350F (175C). Grease a 13" x 9" baking pan. In a large bowl, beat together butter or margarine and brown sugar until fluffy. Add flour, baking soda, salt and cinnamon, beating until blended. Stir in oats. Mixture will be crumbly. Press half of oat mixture evenly in bottom of greased baking pan. In a medium bowl, combine applesauce and raisins or dates. Spread mixture evenly over oat mixture. Sprinkle with walnuts, then with remaining oat mixture, pressing in gently. Bake 25 to 30 minutes or until golden brown. Cool in pan. Cut cooled cookies into bars. Store in refrigerator, if desired. Makes 40 (1-3/4" x 1-1/2") cookies.

Sunshine Squares

Perfect to serve at your next luncheon.

**1/4 cup butter or margarine,
 room temperature**
3/4 cup sugar
1 egg
1 teaspoon milk
1/4 teaspoon salt

1 tablespoon grated orange peel
2/3 cup all-purpose flour
1/2 teaspoon baking powder
1 cup flaked or shredded coconut
**2/3 cup (4 oz.) semisweet chocolate pieces,
 melted**

Preheat oven to 350F (175C). Grease an 8-inch-square baking pan. Line pan with waxed paper; grease paper. In a medium bowl, beat together butter or margarine, sugar, egg, milk, salt and orange peel until light and fluffy. Add flour and baking powder, beating until blended. Stir in coconut. Spread batter evenly in waxed-paper-lined baking pan. Bake 30 minutes or until lightly browned. Cool 5 minutes in pan. Then invert pan of cookies on board. Peel off waxed paper. Spread evenly with melted chocolate. Let stand until set. Refrigerate 1 hour, if desired. Cut cooled cookies into squares. Makes 36 (1-1/4-inch) cookies.

Tip

Baking times are only a guide. When testing for cookie doneness, rely on your instinct and common sense.

How to Make Linzer Squares

1/Divide dough into 2 equal portions. Roll each portion of dough between 2 sheets of waxed paper into an 8-inch square.

2/Place 8 dough strips, 1/2 inch apart, over dough in pan. Place remaining strips over first strips, forming a lattice pattern.

Linzer Squares

A cookie version of the famous Austrian linzer torte, using an almond-paste dough.

**1/4 recipe Basic Almond-Paste Cookie
   Dough, page 117**
1/2 cup raspberry jam

1/2 cup chopped pecans
1 egg yolk
1 teaspoon water

Refrigerate Basic Almond-Paste Cookie Dough at least 1 hour. To bake cookies, preheat oven to 375F (190C). Grease an 8-inch-square baking pan. Divide dough into 2 equal portions. Roll 1 portion between 2 sheets of waxed paper into an 8-inch square. Peel off top sheet of paper; turn dough over into bottom of greased baking pan. Peel off second sheet of paper. Place pan in freezer 5 to 10 minutes to firm dough. Roll remaining portion of dough between 2 sheets of waxed paper into an 8-inch square. Peel off top piece of waxed paper. Cut dough into 16 (1/2-inch-wide) strips. Refrigerate or freeze 10 minutes. In a small bowl, combine jam and pecans. Spread jam mixture over dough in pan to within 1/4 inch of edges. Place 8 dough strips, 1/2 inch apart vertically, over jam. Place remaining 8 dough strips, 1/2 inch apart horizontally, over first strips, forming a lattice pattern. In a small bowl, combine egg yolk and water. Brush egg-yolk mixture on dough strips. Bake 30 to 35 minutes or until top is golden brown. Cool in pan. Cut cooled cookies into squares. Makes about 25 (1-1/2-inch) cookies.

Chocolate-Meringue Bars

Use leftover egg whites in this meringue-topped cookie.

Meringue Topping, see below
1/2 cup butter or margarine,
   room temperature
1/2 cup granulated sugar
1 teaspoon vanilla extract
1/4 cup unsweetened cocoa

1-1/3 cups all-purpose flour
1/2 teaspoon baking powder
1 cup (6 oz.) semisweet chocolate pieces or
   butterscotch-flavor pieces
1 cup chopped almonds or walnuts

Meringue Topping:
3 egg whites
3/4 cup packed brown sugar

Prepare Meringue Topping; set aside. Preheat oven to 350F (175C). Grease a 13" x 9" baking pan. In a medium bowl, beat together butter or margarine, granulated sugar and vanilla until light and fluffy. Add cocoa, flour and baking powder, beating until blended. Press mixture evenly in bottom of greased baking pan. Sprinkle chocolate or butterscotch pieces over crust. Carefully spread with Meringue Topping. Sprinkle with nuts. Bake 30 to 35 minutes or until golden brown. Cool in pan. Cut cooled cookies into bars. Makes 40 (1-3/4" x 1-1/2") cookies.

Meringue Topping:
In a medium bowl, beat egg whites with electric mixer at high speed until foamy. Gradually beat in brown sugar until glossy and stiff peaks form.

Nanaimo Cookie Squares

These triple-layered bars must be kept refrigerated.

1/3 cup butter or margarine, melted
1-1/2 cups graham-cracker crumbs
2 tablespoons granulated sugar
1/3 cup unsweetened cocoa
1 egg
1 teaspoon vanilla extract
1 cup flaked or shredded coconut
1/2 cup chopped walnuts

1/4 cup butter or margarine,
   room temperature
2 cups powdered sugar
3 tablespoons milk
2 tablespoons instant vanilla-pudding and
   pie-filling mix
Fudge Frosting, page 101

Butter an 11" x 7" baking pan. In a medium bowl, combine 1/3 cup melted butter or margarine, graham-cracker crumbs, granulated sugar, cocoa, egg, vanilla, coconut and walnuts, blending well. Press mixture evenly in bottom of buttered baking pan. In a medium bowl, beat together 1/4 cup butter or margarine, powdered sugar, milk and pudding mix until light and fluffy. Spread evenly over top of crumb mixture. Refrigerate until chilled thoroughly. Prepare Fudge Frosting using water instead of milk; cool 5 to 10 minutes. While Fudge Frosting is warm, spread evenly over chilled mixture. Refrigerate overnight. Cut chilled cookies into squares or diamonds. Store in refrigerator. Makes about 40 (1-1/4-inch) cookies.

Congo Bars

These orange-flavored cookies are quick to make.

1/2 cup butter or margarine,
   room temperature
2 cups packed dark-brown sugar
3 eggs
1 teaspoon vanilla extract
2 tablespoons grated orange peel

1/4 teaspoon salt
2-1/2 cups all-purpose flour
2 teaspoons baking powder
3/4 cup chopped walnuts
2 cups (12 oz.) semisweet chocolate pieces

Preheat oven to 350F (175C). Line a 15" x 10" jelly-roll pan with foil. In a large bowl, beat together butter or margarine, brown sugar, eggs, vanilla, orange peel and salt until light and fluffy. Add flour and baking powder, beating until blended. Stir in walnuts and chocolate pieces. Spread batter evenly in foil-lined pan. Bake 20 to 25 minutes or until golden brown. Cool in pan. Cut cooled cookies into bars. Makes about 50 (2" x 1-1/2") cookies.

Variation

Substitute 1 cup (6 ounces) butterscotch-flavor pieces and 1 cup (6 ounces) semisweet chocolate pieces for 2 cups (12 ounces) semisweet chocolate pieces.

Choco-Nut Oat Bars

Sandwich a nut filling between oat-mixture layers for these easy-to-tote bars.

1 (14-oz.) can sweetened condensed milk
2 oz. unsweetened chocolate
1-1/2 cups chopped walnuts, pecans or
   almonds
1 cup butter or margarine, room temperature
1-1/4 cups packed brown sugar

2 teaspoons vanilla extract
2 cups all-purpose flour
1/4 teaspoon salt
1/2 teaspoon baking soda
2-1/2 cups rolled oats

Preheat oven to 375F (190C). Grease a 13" x 9" baking pan. In top of a double boiler, combine sweetened condensed milk and chocolate. Heat over hot but not boiling water until melted and smooth, stirring constantly. Remove from heat. Stir in nuts; set aside. In a medium bowl, beat together butter or margarine, brown sugar and vanilla until light and fluffy. Add flour, salt and baking soda, blending thoroughly. Stir in oats, mixing until crumbly. Press half of oat mixture evenly in bottom of greased baking pan. Spread evenly with chocolate-nut mixture. Sprinkle with remaining oat mixture, pressing into chocolate. Bake 25 to 30 minutes or until golden brown. Cool in pan. Cut cooled cookies into bars. Makes 54 (2" x 1") cookies.

Tip
Sweetened condensed milk and chocolate can be melted together in a 1-quart glass bowl in a microwave oven on full power (HIGH) 1-1/2 to 2-1/2 minutes, stirring twice.

Left to right: Choco-Nut Oat Bars & Congo Bars

Buttery Pecan Sticks

Fragrant with cinnamon and nutmeg, these are good keepers.

1 cup butter or margarine, room temperature
1 cup sugar
1 egg, separated
1 teaspoon vanilla extract
1/4 teaspoon ground nutmeg

1 teaspoon ground cinnamon
2 cups all-purpose flour
3/4 teaspoon baking powder
1-1/4 cups chopped pecans

Preheat oven to 350F (175C). In a medium bowl, beat together butter or margarine, sugar, egg yolk, vanilla, nutmeg and cinnamon until well blended. Gradually beat in flour and baking powder until thoroughly blended. Press mixture evenly in an ungreased 15" x 10" jelly-roll pan. Beat egg white slightly with a fork. Brush over top of dough. Sprinkle evenly with pecans, lightly pressing into dough to secure. Bake 25 to 30 minutes or until golden. Cool 10 minutes in pan; then cut cookies into sticks. Cool completely in pan. Makes 75 (2" x 1") cookies.

Spicy Butterscotch Thins

Crisp thin squares topped with chopped peanuts and butterscotch pieces.

1-1/4 cups (7-1/2 oz.) butterscotch-flavor
  pieces
1/2 cup butter or margarine
1 egg
1/4 cup sugar

3/4 cup all-purpose flour
1 teaspoon ground cinnamon
1/2 teaspoon ground ginger
1 teaspoon instant-coffee powder
1/2 cup chopped salted peanuts

Preheat oven to 300F (150C). Line a 15" x 10" jelly-roll pan with foil. In top of a double boiler, combine 3/4 cup butterscotch pieces and butter or margarine. Heat over hot but not boiling water until melted and smooth, stirring occasionally. Remove from heat. Beat in egg and sugar until blended. Stir in flour, cinnamon, ginger and coffee powder until blended. Batter will be sticky. Spread batter evenly in foil-lined pan. It will be a very thin layer. Sprinkle top evenly with remaining 1/2 cup butterscotch pieces and peanuts. Bake 25 to 30 minutes or until light golden. Cool 2 to 3 minutes in pan; then carefully cut into squares. Cool completely in pan. Makes about 60 (1-1/2-inch) cookies.

Peanut-Butter Bars

Peanut-butter-cup-candy lovers will be in heaven when they taste these.

3/4 cup smooth or crunchy peanut butter,
  room temperature
1 egg white
1/2 cup sugar

2/3 cup chopped unsalted peanuts or walnuts
1 cup (6 oz.) semisweet or
  milk chocolate pieces

Preheat oven to 325F (165C). Grease or line with foil an 11" x 7" baking pan. In a medium bowl, combine peanut butter, egg white and sugar. Stir in nuts. Spread mixture evenly in bottom of greased or foil-lined baking pan. Bake 10 to 12 minutes. Sprinkle chocolate pieces evenly over cookie surface. Bake 2 to 3 minutes or until chocolate melts. Remove from oven and let stand 1 minute. With a knife, spread melted chocolate evenly over top. Cool in pan. Cut cooled cookies into bars. Makes 32 (1-3/4" x 1-1/2") cookies.

Layered Chocolate-Pecan Bars

Full of rich Southern-style praline flavor.

Brown-Sugar Crust, page 96
1/2 cup butter or margarine, melted
1-1/2 cups packed brown sugar
2 eggs
1-1/2 teaspoons vanilla extract

1-1/4 cups all-purpose flour
1-1/2 teaspoons baking powder
1-1/2 cups coarsely chopped pecans
1 cup (6 oz.) semisweet chocolate pieces
48 pecan halves

Preheat oven to 350F (175C). Prepare Brown-Sugar Crust. Press crust mixture evenly in bottom of an ungreased 13" x 9" baking pan. Bake 13 to 15 minutes or until edges are golden. Meanwhile, in a large bowl, combine melted butter or margarine and brown sugar. Add eggs and vanilla, beating until well blended. Beat in flour and baking powder until blended. Stir in chopped pecans. Sprinkle chocolate pieces over hot crust. Bake 2 to 3 minutes or until chocolate melts. Remove from oven and let stand 1 minute. With a knife, spread melted chocolate over baked crust. Top melted chocolate with pecan mixture, spreading evenly. Arrange pecan halves on filling in 6 rows of 8, spacing evenly. Bake 23 to 25 minutes or until golden. Cool in pan. Cut cooled cookies into 48 squares with a pecan half in center of each. Makes 48 (1-1/2-inch) cookies.

White-Chocolate Brownies Supreme

White chocolate gives a special flavor. Serve as an accompaniment to fresh fruit.

12 oz. white chocolate, cut in pieces
1/3 cup butter or margarine
1 cup sugar
3 eggs
1 teaspoon vanilla extract

2 teaspoons grated orange peel
1-1/4 cups all-purpose flour
1/2 teaspoon baking powder
3/4 cup chopped pecans

Preheat oven to 350F (175C). Grease an 11" x 7" baking pan or a 9-inch-square baking pan. In top of a double boiler, combine half the white chocolate and butter or margarine. Heat over hot but not boiling water until melted and smooth, stirring occasionally. Remove from heat. Add sugar, eggs, vanilla and orange peel, beating until blended. Stir in flour and baking powder, blending well. Stir in pecans. Spread mixture evenly in greased baking pan. Bake 23 to 25 minutes or until light golden. Do not overbake or brownies will be dry. Cool in pan. Meanwhile, in top of double boiler, melt remaining white chocolate over hot but not boiling water. Spread melted chocolate evenly over brownies. Let stand until set. Cut cooled brownies into bars. Makes 20 (2-1/4" x 1-3/4") brownies.

Tip *For very moist brownies, use the white-chocolate-coating wafers available in cake- and candy-decorating-supply stores.*

Cherry Bars

Made to order for maraschino-cherry fanciers.

1-1/4 cups all-purpose flour	3/4 cup granulated sugar
1/4 cup powdered sugar	2 eggs
1/2 cup butter or margarine	1/2 cup chopped maraschino cherries
1/2 teaspoon baking powder	1/2 cup flaked or shredded coconut
1/4 teaspoon salt	1/2 cup chopped walnuts

Preheat oven to 350F (175C). In a medium bowl, combine 1 cup flour and powdered sugar. Using a fork or pastry blender, cut in butter or margarine until mixture resembles coarse crumbs. Press mixture evenly in bottom of an ungreased 11" x 7" baking pan. Bake 10 minutes. Meanwhile, in a medium bowl, combine remaining 1/4 cup flour, baking powder, salt and granulated sugar. Add eggs; stir well. Stir in cherries, coconut and walnuts. Spread mixture evenly over baked crust. Bake 20 minutes or until golden brown. Cool in pan. Cut cooled cookies into bars. Makes 44 (1-3/4" x 1") cookies.

Toffee Squares

One of my mother's all-time favorites. These cookies are best served chilled.

1 cup butter or margarine, room temperature	2 cups all-purpose flour
1 cup packed brown sugar	1 cup (6 oz.) semisweet chocolate pieces
1 egg yolk	1 cup chopped walnuts
1 teaspoon vanilla extract	

Preheat oven to 350F (175C). Line a 15" x 10" jelly-roll pan with foil. In a medium bowl, beat together butter or margarine, brown sugar, egg yolk and vanilla until light and fluffy. Add flour, beating until well blended. Spread mixture evenly in foil-lined pan. Bake 15 to 18 minutes or until golden. Sprinkle chocolate pieces evenly over cookie surface. Bake 2 to 3 minutes or until chocolate melts. Remove from oven and let stand 1 minute. With a knife, spread melted chocolate evenly over top. Sprinkle with walnuts. While warm, cut into squares. Cool in pan. Store in refrigerator, if desired. Makes about 54 (1-5/8-inch) cookies.

Nutty Tart Squares

Rich and elegant with three kinds of nuts.

Brown-Sugar Crust, page 96	1/2 cup pecan halves
2/3 cup sugar	1/2 cup coarsely chopped walnuts
2/3 cup whipping cream	1/3 cup blanched sliced almonds
1/4 teaspoon orange extract	

Preheat oven to 350F (175C). Prepare Brown-Sugar Crust. Press crust mixture evenly in bottom of an ungreased 8- or 9-inch-square baking pan. Bake 13 to 15 minutes or until edges are golden. In a medium bowl, combine sugar, cream, orange extract and nuts with a fork. Pour mixture evenly over baked crust. Bake 40 to 45 minutes longer or until golden brown. Cool in pan. Cut cooled cookies into squares. Store in refrigerator. Makes 25 (1-1/2-inch) cookies.

Surprise Bars

An irresistible variation on the layered-bar theme.

3/4 cup butter or margarine,
   room temperature
3/4 cup sugar
3 tablespoons molasses
1 egg yolk
1 teaspoon vanilla extract

1-3/4 cups all-purpose flour
3 cups (18 oz.) semisweet chocolate pieces
1/3 cup crunchy peanut butter
3/4 cup currants
1 cup chopped dry-roasted peanuts or walnuts

Preheat oven to 350F (175C). In a large bowl, beat together butter or margarine, sugar, molasses, egg yolk and vanilla until blended. Beat in flour. Stir in 1 cup chocolate pieces. Press mixture in bottom of an ungreased 13" x 9" baking pan. Bake 25 to 30 minutes or until golden brown. Meanwhile, in a medium saucepan, combine remaining 2 cups chocolate pieces and peanut butter. Heat over low heat until melted, stirring occasionally. Stir in currants and nuts. Spread mixture over warm crust. Cool in pan; then refrigerate at least 2 hours. Cut chilled cookies into bars. Makes about 54 (2" x 1") cookies.

Rum Refrigerator Brownies

These require no baking and should be kept refrigerated.

1 cup chopped walnuts
2 cups miniature marshmallows
2-3/4 cups graham-cracker crumbs
1 cup powdered sugar

2 cups (12 oz.) semisweet chocolate pieces
1 cup evaporated milk
1/4 teaspoon salt
1-1/2 teaspoons rum extract

Butter an 8- or 9-inch-square baking pan. In a large bowl, combine walnuts, marshmallows, graham-cracker crumbs and powdered sugar; set aside. In a medium saucepan, combine chocolate pieces and evaporated milk. Heat over low heat until melted and smooth, stirring constantly. Remove from heat and stir in salt and rum extract. Remove 1/2 cup chocolate mixture; set aside. Mix remaining chocolate mixture with graham-cracker-crumb mixture until all crumbs are moistened. Turn into buttered baking pan, pressing down to fill pan evenly. Spread with reserved chocolate mixture. Refrigerate in pan. Cut chilled cookies into squares. Store in refrigerator. Makes 25 (1-1/2-inch) cookies.

Ways with Coconut

Tint coconut assorted colors for decorating cutout cookies, especially at Easter or holiday time. To tint coconut, mix 1/2 teaspoon water and a few drops of food coloring in a bowl. Add about 1 to 1-1/3 cups flaked or shredded coconut. Toss with a fork until coconut is evenly tinted. Or, place coconut in a food processor. Add a few drops of food coloring on top of coconut. Process until evenly colored. To make chocolate coconut, heat 2 ounces semisweet chocolate in top of a double boiler until melted. Add about 1-1/3 cups flaked or shredded coconut; stir well. Spread on a baking sheet, separating with fork. Chill until chocolate is set. Store in a tightly covered jar. To toast coconut, spread in a shallow pan and bake at 350F (175C) 7 to 10 minutes or until lightly brown, stirring often.

Drop Cookies

When the cookie jar is overflowing, generally you will find the drop variety. One reason is because next to bar cookies, drop cookies are one of the easiest kinds to prepare. Although some bakers find dropping the dough onto baking sheets drudgery, it doesn't have to be. Fit such tasks between other daily chores or encourage children to assist.

Customize your drop cookies by making them very small or saucer-size or anywhere in between. If your children are like mine, they'll appreciate having a single giant cookie tucked in their lunch box for a change of pace.

These recipes are, for the most part, simple and plain. There's nothing better for replenishing the cookie jar. Most can be made quickly.

A general rule for drop cookies is to space them about two inches apart on baking sheets. Keep drop cookies uniform in size and shape for even baking. When making drop cookies, working with more than one baking sheet will save time.

Ever thought of having cookies for breakfast? Now you can with tailor-made tasty Get-Up-&-Go Breakfast Cookies loaded with crisp crumbled bacon, chewy cereal and flavored with orange peel and juice. Stored in the refrigerator, they are great for grabbing on-the-run.

When your garden is overflowing with zucchini, try the recipe for Zucchini Drops. It may become one of your most requested drop-cookie recipes. My daughter rated these easy cookies as one of her all-time favorites.

Fall and winter bring with them special fruits and cookies. Cranberry Softies utilize fresh or frozen cranberries in combination with orange peel. Persimmon Drop Cookies team persimmon pulp with a blend of spices, coconut, dates and almonds for some terrific eating.

Who said drop cookies can't be magnificent? One of the most dazzling cookie recipes is Lacy Almond-Sesame Crisps. Serve them individually, frosted with melted chocolate or sandwiched together with raspberry jam. They are simply divine.

Oatmeal-Raisin Cookies

Large and chewy, these are favorites with the young set.

1/2 cup butter or margarine,
 room temperature
1/2 cup vegetable shortening
1 cup packed brown sugar
3/4 cup granulated sugar
2 eggs
2 teaspoons vanilla extract
1-3/4 cups all-purpose flour

1/2 teaspoon salt
1 teaspoon baking soda
1 teaspoon baking powder
2 cups rolled oats
1-1/2 cups raisins
1/2 cup flaked or shredded coconut,
 if desired

Preheat oven to 350F (175C). In a large bowl, beat together butter or margarine, shortening, brown sugar, granulated sugar, eggs and vanilla until light and fluffy. Gradually beat in flour, salt, baking soda and baking powder until thoroughly blended. Stir in oats, raisins and coconut, if desired. Drop by rounded tablespoonfuls, 3 inches apart, on ungreased baking sheets. Bake 13 to 15 minutes or until lightly browned. Remove cookies from baking sheets; cool on racks. Makes about 38 (3-inch) cookies.

Variation

Delete raisins and add 1-1/2 cups chopped walnuts. Or, reduce raisins to 3/4 cup and add 3/4 cup chopped walnuts.

Get-Up-&-Go Breakfast Cookies   *Photo on page 42.*

Highlighted with bacon, cereal and orange peel—great for breakfast on-the-run.

1/2 cup butter or margarine,
 room temperature
1/2 cup sugar
1 egg
2 tablespoons thawed frozen-orange-juice
 concentrate
1 tablespoon grated orange peel

1-1/4 cups all-purpose flour
1 teaspoon baking powder
1/2 lb. bacon, cooked crisp, drained,
 crumbled
1/2 cup wheat and barley cereal,
 such as Grape-Nuts

Preheat oven to 350F (175C). In a medium bowl, beat together butter or margarine, sugar, egg, orange-juice concentrate and orange peel until light and fluffy. Add flour and baking powder, beating until well blended. Stir in bacon and cereal. Drop by teaspoonfuls, 2 inches apart, on ungreased baking sheets. Bake 10 to 12 minutes or until edges are golden. Remove cookies from baking sheets; cool on racks. Store in refrigerator. Makes about 40 (1-3/4-inch) cookies.

Variation

Cheesy Breakfast Cookies: Stir in 1 cup shredded Cheddar cheese (4 ounces) along with bacon and cereal. Bake on lightly greased baking sheets. Proceed as directed above.

Tip

When dropping cookie dough by teaspoonfuls, use a tableware teaspoon, not a measuring teaspoon.

Banana Drop Cookies

Bake these cake-like cookies when you have soft ripe bananas.

3/4 cup butter or margarine,
  room temperature
3/4 cup packed brown sugar
2 eggs
1 teaspoon vanilla extract
1 cup mashed bananas (about 3 medium)
1-1/2 teaspoons ground cinnamon

1/2 teaspoon ground nutmeg
2-1/4 cups all-purpose flour
2 teaspoons baking powder
1/4 teaspoon baking soda
1/2 cup chopped walnuts, if desired
1/2 cup raisins, if desired

Preheat oven to 350F (175C). Grease baking sheets. In a large bowl, beat together butter or margarine, brown sugar, eggs and vanilla until light and fluffy. Beat in bananas, cinnamon and nutmeg. Add flour, baking powder and baking soda, beating until blended. Stir in walnuts and raisins, if desired. Dough will be sticky. Drop by rounded teaspoonfuls, 2 inches apart, on greased baking sheets. Bake 12 to 14 minutes or until golden. Remove cookies from baking sheets; cool on racks. Makes about 54 (2-inch) cookies.

Cranberry Softies

Soft cookies tangy with bits of fresh or frozen cranberries and flavored with orange peel.

1/4 cup butter or margarine,
  room temperature
3/4 cup packed brown sugar
1 egg
1 teaspoon vanilla extract
1 tablespoon grated orange peel

Pinch of salt
1-1/2 cups all-purpose flour
1/2 teaspoon baking soda
1/2 cup chopped walnuts
3/4 cup chopped fresh or
  thawed frozen cranberries

Preheat oven to 375F (190C). Grease baking sheets. In a medium bowl, beat together butter or margarine, brown sugar, egg, vanilla, orange peel and salt until light and fluffy. Add flour and baking soda, beating until well blended. Stir in walnuts. Carefully fold in cranberries. Drop by rounded teaspoonfuls, 2 inches apart, on greased baking sheets. Bake 10 to 12 minutes or until golden. Remove from baking sheets; cool on racks. Makes about 48 (1-3/4-inch) cookies.

Orange-Carrot Cookies

Nutritious, moist cookies bursting with carrots.

1 cup butter or margarine,
  room temperature
1/2 cup packed brown sugar
1 egg
1 teaspoon vanilla extract
1 tablespoon grated orange peel

1 cup finely shredded raw carrot
2 cups all-purpose flour
2 teaspoons baking powder
3/4 cup flaked or shredded coconut
1 cup granola or chopped walnuts

Preheat oven to 375F (190C). Grease baking sheets. In a large bowl, beat butter or margarine, sugar, egg, vanilla and orange peel until fluffy. Stir in carrot. Add flour and baking powder, beating until blended. Stir in coconut and granola or nuts. Drop by heaping teaspoonfuls, 1-1/2 inches apart, on greased baking sheets. Bake 10 to 12 minutes or until bottoms are lightly browned. Remove cookies from baking sheets; cool on racks. Makes about 75 (1-1/2-inch) cookies.

Fruitcake Drops   *Photo on pages 154 and 155*

Miniature fruitcake cookies require no aging, so you can enjoy fruitcake in short order.

1/2 cup butter or margarine,
　room temperature
1/2 cup packed brown sugar
1 egg
Pinch of salt
2 tablespoons brandy or rum
1-1/2 cups all-purpose flour
1/2 teaspoon baking soda

1/2 teaspoon ground cinnamon
1/8 teaspoon ground nutmeg
2-1/2 cups chopped pecans or walnuts
1 cup chopped pitted dates
1 cup chopped candied pineapple
1/2 cup chopped red candied cherries
1/2 cup chopped green candied cherries

Preheat oven to 350F (175C). Grease baking sheets. In a large bowl, beat together butter or margarine, brown sugar, egg, salt and brandy or rum until light and fluffy. Add flour, baking soda, cinnamon and nutmeg, beating until blended. Stir in nuts, dates, candied pineapple and candied cherries. Drop by teaspoonfuls, 1-1/2 inches apart, on greased baking sheets. Bake 14 to 15 minutes or until lightly browned. Cool 2 to 3 minutes on baking sheets; then remove to racks to cool completely. Makes about 85 (1-1/2-inch) cookies.

Persimmon Drop Cookies

During persimmon season, bake these delicious moist cookies; then freeze to enjoy at a later date.

1 cup persimmon pulp
1 teaspoon baking soda
1/2 cup butter or margarine,
　room temperature
3/4 cup sugar
1 egg
2 teaspoons grated orange peel
1/4 teaspoon salt

2-1/4 cups all-purpose flour
1/2 teaspoon ground cinnamon
1/2 teaspoon ground cloves
1/2 teaspoon ground nutmeg
1/2 cup chopped pitted dates
1/2 cup flaked or shredded coconut
1 cup toasted chopped unblanched almonds

Preheat oven to 350F (175C). Grease baking sheets. In a small bowl, combine persimmon pulp and baking soda; set aside. In a large bowl, beat together butter or margarine, sugar, egg, orange peel and salt until creamy. Beat in persimmon mixture. Add flour, cinnamon, cloves and nutmeg, beating until blended. Stir in dates, coconut and almonds. Drop by teaspoonfuls, 1-1/2 inches apart, on greased baking sheets. Bake 10 to 13 minutes or until edges are golden. Remove cookies from baking sheets; cool on racks. Makes 80 (1-1/2-inch) cookies.

Tip

Quick-cooking and old-fashioned oats can be used interchangeably in these recipes. If desired, oats can be toasted at 300F (150C) 8 to 10 minutes. This will give improved texture and flavor.

Pumpkin Drops

At Halloween, make these with cooked fresh pumpkin.

3/4 cup butter or margarine,
   room temperature
2/3 cup packed brown sugar
2 eggs
1-1/2 teaspoons vanilla extract
1 cup canned or cooked fresh pumpkin
2 cups all-purpose flour

1/2 teaspoon baking powder
1/2 teaspoon baking soda
Pinch of salt
2-1/2 teaspoons pumpkin-pie spice
1 cup raisins, or chopped pitted dates or
   prunes
1 cup chopped walnuts

Preheat oven to 375F (190C). In a large bowl, beat together butter or margarine, brown sugar, eggs and vanilla until light and fluffy. Beat in pumpkin. Add flour, baking powder, baking soda, salt and pumpkin-pie spice, beating until blended. Stir in raisins, dates or prunes and walnuts. Drop by teaspoonfuls, 2 inches apart, on ungreased baking sheets. Bake 10 to 12 minutes or until edges are golden. Remove cookies from baking sheets; cool on racks. Makes about 80 (1-1/2-inch) cookies.

Spiced Applesauce Drops

Applesauce spiced with cinnamon and cloves flavors these soft cookies.

1/4 cup butter or margarine,
   room temperature
1/4 cup vegetable shortening
1-1/4 cups packed brown sugar
2 eggs
1 teaspoon vanilla extract
3/4 cup unsweetened applesauce

2-3/4 cups all-purpose flour
1 teaspoon baking soda
1 teaspoon ground cinnamon
1/4 teaspoon ground cloves
1 cup raisins or chopped pitted dates
1 cup chopped walnuts

Preheat oven to 375F (190C). Lightly grease baking sheets. In a large bowl, beat together butter or margarine, shortening, brown sugar, eggs and vanilla until light and fluffy. Beat in applesauce. Add flour, baking soda, cinnamon and cloves, beating until blended. Stir in raisins or dates and walnuts. Drop by teaspoonfuls, 2 inches apart, on greased baking sheets. Bake 10 minutes or until almost no imprint remains when touched with your finger. Remove cookies from baking sheets; cool on racks. Makes about 65 (1-3/4-inch) cookies.

Tip

Avoid overbaking cookies. Check them a few minutes prior to the minimum baking time suggested in the recipe.

How to Make Lacy Almond-Sesame Crisps

1/Drop dough by half-teaspoonfuls, 3 inches apart, on foil-lined baking sheets.

2/Sandwich 2 cookies together with jam. Spread half of top side with melted chocolate.

Lacy Almond-Sesame Crisps

Crisp and fragile, these are delicious sandwiched together with raspberry jam.

6 tablespoons butter
1/3 cup packed brown sugar
3 tablespoons light corn syrup
1/3 cup all-purpose flour
1/2 cup ground blanched almonds

3 to 4 tablespoons sesame seeds
1 teaspoon vanilla extract
About 1/3 cup raspberry jam
2/3 cup (4 oz.) semisweet chocolate pieces, melted

Preheat oven to 350F (175C). Line baking sheets with foil. **Do not grease.** In a medium saucepan, combine butter, brown sugar and corn syrup. Cook over medium heat until butter melts and mixture boils, stirring constantly. Remove from heat. All at once, stir in flour, almonds and sesame seeds until thoroughly blended. Stir in vanilla. Drop by half-teaspoonfuls, 3 inches apart, on foil-lined baking sheets. It will look like a very small amount of dough. Cookies need plenty of room for spreading. Bake 6 to 8 minutes or until a rich golden color. Cool 5 minutes on baking sheets before carefully peeling off foil. Place cookies on cooling racks to cool completely. When cool, sandwich 2 cookies, bottom sides together, with a thin layer of jam between. Spread half of top side of each cookie sandwich with melted chocolate. Let stand until chocolate has set. Store in refrigerator. Makes 30 to 32 (2- to 2-1/2-inch) filled cookies.

Variation

Omit sandwiching cookies together with jam. Spread bottoms of single cookies with 1-1/3 cups (8 ounces) semisweet chocolate pieces, melted. Makes 60 to 64 (2- to 2-1/2-inch) cookies.

Sour-Cream Cookies

Delicate drops sprinkled with cinnamon-sugar appeal to all.

1/2 cup vegetable shortening
2 cups sugar
2 eggs
1 teaspoon vanilla extract
4 cups all-purpose flour

1/2 teaspoon salt
1 teaspoon baking soda
1 cup dairy sour cream
1 tablespoon ground cinnamon
2 tablespoons sugar

Preheat oven to 375F (190C). Grease baking sheets. In a large bowl, beat together shortening and 2 cups sugar until creamy. Beat in eggs and vanilla. In a medium bowl, combine flour, salt and baking soda. Add flour mixture to egg mixture alternately with sour cream; blend well. Drop by teaspoonfuls, 2 inches apart, on greased baking sheets. In a small bowl, combine cinnamon and 2 tablespoons sugar. Sprinkle cinnamon mixture over cookies. Bake 12 to 15 minutes or until bottoms are golden. Remove cookies from baking sheets; cool on racks. Makes about 80 (1-1/2-inch) cookies.

Fudgy Chocolate Drops

Rich and loaded with chocolate—perfect for chocoholics.

2 cups (12 oz.) semisweet chocolate pieces
2 oz. unsweetened chocolate
3 tablespoons butter
1/2 cup sugar
1 egg

2 teaspoons rum extract
1/3 cup all-purpose flour
1/4 teaspoon baking powder
Pinch of salt
1 cup chopped walnuts

Preheat oven to 350F (175C). In top of a double boiler, combine 1-1/2 cups semisweet chocolate pieces, unsweetened chocolate and butter. Heat over hot but not boiling water until melted and smooth, stirring occasionally; cool slightly. Stir in sugar, egg and rum extract. Add flour, baking powder and salt, blending thoroughly. Stir in remaining 1/2 cup chocolate pieces and walnuts. Shape into 1-1/4-inch balls or drop by teaspoonfuls, 1-1/2 inches apart, on ungreased baking sheets. Bake 8 to 10 minutes, no longer. Cookies will be soft. Cool 5 minutes on baking sheets, then remove to racks to cool completely. Makes about 50 (1-1/2-inch) cookies.

Almond Meringues   Photo on page 103.

Light and airy, these are reminiscent of French macaroons. Top with melted chocolate, if desired.

3 egg whites
1/4 teaspoon cream of tartar
1/2 teaspoon vanilla or almond extract
3/4 cup sugar

1-1/2 cups finely ground blanched almonds
2 oz. semisweet chocolate, melted,
   if desired

Preheat oven to 350F (175C). Line 2 baking sheets with foil. In a medium bowl, beat egg whites and cream of tartar with electric mixer at high speed until frothy, adding vanilla or almond extract toward the end of beating. Beat in sugar until stiff. Fold in almonds, half at a time. Drop by teaspoonfuls, 1 inch apart, on foil-lined baking sheets. Or, pipe through a pastry bag. Bake 13 to 15 minutes or until light golden. Cool 5 minutes on baking sheets; then remove to racks to cool completely. Spread or pipe tops of cooled cookies with melted chocolate, if desired. Makes about 30 (1-3/4-inch) cookies.

Back to front: Get-Up-&-Go Breakfast Cookies, page 37; Fudgy Chocolate Drops, above; and Sour-Cream Cookies, above.

43

How to Make Zucchini Drops

1/Coarsely grate unpeeled zucchini.

2/Drop dough with a teaspoon or cookie dropper.

Zucchini Drops

My daughter enjoys these moist and flavorful cookies; a good way to use fresh zucchini.

1 cup butter or margarine, room temperature
1 cup packed brown sugar
1 egg
1-1/2 teaspoons vanilla extract
1 cup grated unpeeled raw zucchini
2 to 2-1/4 cups all-purpose flour
1 teaspoon baking powder

1 teaspoon baking soda
1-1/2 teaspoons ground cinnamon
1-1/2 teaspoons ground nutmeg
Pinch of salt
1 cup flaked or shredded coconut
1 cup chopped walnuts

Preheat oven to 350F (175C). In a large bowl, beat together butter or margarine, brown sugar, egg and vanilla until light and fluffy. Stir in zucchini. Add 2 cups flour, baking powder, baking soda, cinnamon, nutmeg and salt, beating until thoroughly blended. Add additional flour, if needed, depending on wetness of zucchini. Stir in coconut and walnuts. Drop by teaspoonfuls, 2 inches apart, on ungreased baking sheets. Bake 10 to 12 minutes or until lightly browned. Remove cookies from baking sheets; cool on racks. Makes about 72 (2-inch) cookies.

Hermits

A spicy drop cookie dating back to clipper-ship days; great to pack for travel.

1/2 cup butter or margarine, room temperature	Pinch of salt
3/4 cup packed brown sugar	1 teaspoon ground cinnamon
1 egg	1/4 teaspoon ground nutmeg
2 teaspoons instant-coffee powder	1/4 teaspoon ground cloves
1-1/2 cups all-purpose flour	1 cup raisins
1/2 teaspoon baking soda	3/4 cup chopped walnuts

Preheat oven to 375F (190C). In a medium bowl, beat together butter or margarine, brown sugar, egg and coffee powder until fluffy. Add flour, baking soda, salt, cinnamon, nutmeg and cloves, beating until blended. Stir in raisins and walnuts. Drop by teaspoonfuls, 2 inches apart, on ungreased baking sheets. Bake 8 to 10 minutes or until bottoms are lightly browned. Remove cookies from baking sheets; cool on racks. Makes about 48 (1-3/4-inch) cookies.

Chocolate-Coconutty Chews

These bring back fond childhood memories.

1 (14-oz.) can sweetened condensed milk	2 teaspoons vanilla extract
2 oz. unsweetened chocolate	1-1/2 cups flaked or shredded coconut
Pinch of salt	1-1/2 cups coarsely chopped pecans

Preheat oven to 325F (165C). Line baking sheets with foil; grease foil generously. In top of a double boiler, combine sweetened condensed milk and chocolate. Place over boiling water on medium-high to high heat. Cook until mixture thickens, about 6 minutes, stirring frequently. Stir in salt and vanilla. Stir in coconut and pecans. Drop by teaspoonfuls, about 2 inches apart, on greased, foil-lined baking sheets. Bake 12 to 14 minutes or until edges begin to brown. Watch carefully to avoid burning. Cookies will be very soft, but will become firm as they cool. Cool 5 minutes on baking sheets; then carefully remove to racks to cool completely. Makes about 48 (1-1/4-inch) cookies.

Variation

Chocolate-Pecan Chews: Delete coconut and increase pecans to 2 cups. Proceed as directed above.

Tip

To speed baking, work with two or three baking sheets at a time.

Refrigerator Cookies

Formerly known as *icebox cookies,* these old-timers rate high in popularity with busy cooks. Creating refrigerator cookies is a two-step procedure—great when only short blocks of time are available. You'll find this type of cookie ideal for fitting in between appointments, car pools, meetings and other activities. One day you can mix, shape, wrap and refrigerate the dough. When you have time a little later—several hours, a day or up to a week—you can bake the cookies. If you don't plan to bake the dough within a week, freeze it in moisture- and vapor-proof paper or freezer bags. Bake within one to two months. Most dough rolls cut best if sliced about 1/4 inch thick with a sharp knife. If cut thinner, the dough will often crumble or break. Be sure to cut all cookies the same thickness so they'll be done in the same amount of time.

Some recipes call for rolling the dough log in chopped nuts or coconut. To do so, simply spread nuts or coconut in a row, the length of the dough. Then coat the log completely. When you bake them, the edges will be fancy.

What are some of the prettiest refrigerator-style cookies? Rainbow Slices may remind you of Neapolitan ice cream with the brown, pink and white layers, each flavored a bit differently. Linzer Rounds are buttery rich and loaded with nuts. Put two of the delicate rounds together with currant jelly between. With a dusting of powdered sugar, they are an elegant and complementary addition to any cookie tray.

For a delicious tender cookie prepared with whole-wheat pastry flour, try Nutty Whole-Wheat Refrigerator Slices. With almonds or hazelnuts, you'll find them a pleasant surprise—and a cookie you'll want to make often.

In case you want to toss in some savory wafers with all of the sweet, Cheese Wafers are superb. You can enjoy them with morning coffee, afternoon tea or simply as an hors d'oeuvre.

Crisp and thin, any or all of these refrigerator cookies are ideal to serve alongside ice cream, sherbets, iced tea, lemonade, coffee, milk and punch. Combine several of them on a festive tray of cookie treats.

English Tea Cookies

Excellent served with lemonade or milk.

1 cup butter or margarine, room temperature
2 cups packed brown sugar
2 eggs
2 teaspoons vanilla extract

3-1/2 cups all-purpose flour
1 tablespoon baking powder
Granulated sugar, if desired

In a large bowl, beat together butter or margarine, brown sugar, eggs and vanilla until light and fluffy. Add flour and baking powder, beating until blended. Dough will be stiff. Divide dough into 4 equal portions. Shape each portion into a log 7 inches long and 1-3/4 inches in diameter. Wrap and refrigerate until firm, several hours or overnight. To bake cookies, preheat oven to 375F (190C). Lightly grease baking sheets. Cut chilled dough into 1/4-inch slices. Place 2 inches apart on greased baking sheets. Sprinkle with granulated sugar, if desired. Bake 8 to 10 minutes or until golden. Remove cookies from baking sheets; cool on racks. Makes about 104 (2-1/4-inch) cookies.

Nutty Whole-Wheat Refrigerator Slices

Crispy cookies with the special flavor of toasted blanched almonds or hazelnuts.

1/2 cup butter or margarine,
room temperature
1/2 cup sugar

3/4 cup finely ground, toasted
blanched almonds
1 cup whole-wheat pastry flour

In a medium bowl, beat together butter or margarine and sugar until creamy. Add almonds. Gradually beat in flour until thoroughly blended. Shape dough into a log 7 inches long and 2 inches in diameter. Wrap and refrigerate until firm, at least 1 hour. To bake cookies, preheat oven to 350F (175C). Cut chilled dough into 1/4-inch slices. Place 1-1/2 inches apart on an ungreased baking sheet. Bake 10 to 12 minutes or until golden. Cool 5 minutes on baking sheet; then remove to racks to cool completely. Makes about 24 (2-1/2-inch) cookies.

Variation

Hazelnut Cookies: Substitute 3/4 cup finely ground toasted hazelnuts or filberts for almonds. Toast whole hazelnuts at 350F (175C) in a toaster oven or conventional oven 10 minutes. Cool. Remove skins from hazelnuts by rubbing them between palms of your hands in a terry-cloth towel. Rub off as much of the skins as possible—it's impossible to get them all off. In a blender or food processor fitted with steel blade, process hazelnuts until finely ground. Measure and use as directed above.

Tip

Regular whole-wheat flour can be used, but cookies will not be as light as when made with pastry flour.

Linzer Rounds

An extremely delicate European-style cookie sandwich.

3/4 cup unsalted butter, room temperature
2/3 cup granulated sugar
1 egg
1 teaspoon vanilla extract
1/2 teaspoon grated lemon peel

1-1/2 cups finely ground walnuts
2 cups all-purpose flour
Powdered sugar
2/3 cup currant jelly

In a large bowl, beat together butter, granulated sugar, egg, vanilla and lemon peel until light and fluffy. Add walnuts and flour, beating until blended. Divide dough into 2 equal portions. Shape each portion into a log 14 inches long and 1-1/4 inches in diameter. Wrap and refrigerate until firm, several hours or overnight. To bake cookies, preheat oven to 325F (165C). Lightly grease baking sheets. Cut chilled dough into 3/16-inch slices. Place 1 inch apart on greased baking sheets. In center of half the unbaked slices, cut a small 3/8-inch hole using tip of a decorating tube. Bake 10 minutes or until golden. Cool 1 to 2 minutes on baking sheets; then remove to waxed paper on a flat surface to cool completely. Sprinkle powdered sugar over tops of cooled cookies with holes. Spread scant 1/2 teaspoon jelly over bottoms of cooled cookies without holes; then top each with a cookie with a hole in it, powdered-sugar-side up. Makes about 65 (1-1/2-inch) cookies.

Raspberry Swirls   *Photo on page 52.*

Superb tasting and very attractive. Make these pinwheels when you want something special.

1/2 cup butter or margarine,
   room temperature
1 cup sugar
1 teaspoon vanilla extract
1 egg
2 cups all-purpose flour

1 teaspoon baking powder
1/4 teaspoon salt
1/2 cup raspberry jam
1/2 cup flaked or shredded coconut
1/4 cup finely chopped walnuts

In a medium bowl, beat together butter or margarine, sugar, vanilla and egg until light and fluffy. Add flour, baking powder and salt, beating until blended. Refrigerate until firm, several hours or overnight. Before rolling out dough, let stand at room temperature until soft enough to roll easily. On a lightly floured surface, roll dough into a 12" x 9" rectangle. In a small bowl, combine jam, coconut and walnuts. Spread jam mixture evenly over dough to within 1/2 inch of edges. Roll up dough, jelly-roll fashion, from long side. Cut log in half for ease in handling. Wrap and refrigerate until firm, several hours or overnight. To bake cookies, preheat oven to 375F (190C). Grease baking sheets. Cut chilled dough into 1/4-inch slices. Place 2 inches apart on greased baking sheets. Bake 8 to 10 minutes or until edges are golden. Remove cookies from baking sheets; cool on racks. Makes about 45 (1-3/4-inch) cookies.

Tip
To avoid round edges on refrigerator cookies and avoid losing the end cookie, flatten the ends of the refrigerator-cookie roll by standing it on end. Strike on the counter a few times. Do before or after chilling, depending on the consistency of the dough.

Peanut-Butter & Chocolate Go-Rounds

Easier to make than they look.

**1 recipe Peanut-Butter-Cookie Cutouts
   dough, page 116**

**1 cup (6 oz.) semisweet chocolate pieces,
   melted**

Divide Peanut-Butter-Cookie Cutouts dough into 2 equal portions. Wrap and refrigerate until firm, 2 to 3 hours. On lightly floured waxed paper, roll 1 portion into an 11" x 7" rectangle. Spread rectangle with half the melted chocolate to within 1/2 inch of edges. Roll up dough, jelly-roll fashion, from long side. Repeat with remaining dough and chocolate. Wrap and refrigerate until firm, several hours or overnight. To bake cookies, preheat oven to 375F (190C). Cut chilled dough into 1/4-inch slices. Place 1 inch apart on ungreased baking sheets. Bake 8 to 10 minutes or only until golden. Watch carefully to avoid overbaking. Remove cookies from baking sheets; cool on racks. Makes about 80 (1-3/4-inch) cookies.

Fig Pinwheels

Dried figs fill these traditional swirled cookies.

Fig Filling, see below
**1/2 cup butter or margarine,
   room temperature**
1/2 cup packed brown sugar
1/2 cup granulated sugar

1 egg
1 teaspoon vanilla extract
1-3/4 cups all-purpose flour
1/2 teaspoon baking soda

Fig Filling:
**1 (8-oz.) pkg. dried figs, stems removed,
   chopped**
1/2 cup water

1/4 cup granulated sugar
1 teaspoon grated lemon peel
1/2 cup finely chopped walnuts

Prepare Fig Filling; set aside to cool. In a medium bowl, beat together butter or margarine, brown sugar, granulated sugar, egg and vanilla until light and fluffy. Add flour and baking soda, beating until blended. Divide dough into 2 equal portions. On lightly floured waxed paper, roll each portion into an 11" x 7" rectangle. Spread each rectangle with half the Fig Filling to within 1/2 inch of edges. Roll up dough, jelly-roll fashion, from long side. Wrap and refrigerate until firm, several hours or overnight. To bake cookies, preheat oven to 375F (190C). Cut chilled dough into 1/4-inch slices. Place 1 inch apart on ungreased baking sheets. Bake 8 to 9 minutes or until light golden. Remove cookies from baking sheets; cool on racks. Makes about 85 (1-3/4-inch) cookies.

Fig Filling:
In a medium saucepan, combine figs, water and granulated sugar. Bring to a boil, stirring constantly. Reduce heat to medium; cook until thickened, 3 to 5 minutes, stirring often. Remove from heat. Stir in lemon peel and walnuts.

Variation

Date-Nut Pinwheels: Prepare recipe as directed, substituting Date-Nut Filling for Fig Filling. To make Date-Nut Filling, in a medium saucepan, combine 1 (8-ounce) package chopped pitted dates and 1/4 cup water. Bring to a boil, stirring constantly. Reduce heat to medium; cover and cook until thickened, 3 to 5 minutes, stirring occasionally. Remove from heat. Stir in 3/4 cup finely chopped walnuts and 1 tablespoon grated orange peel.

Two-Tone Cookie Roll

Surround a chocolate-nut center with a buttery cookie dough for an attractive cookie.

Chocolate-Nut Log Center, see below
1 recipe Basic Butter-Cookie Dough,
　　page 117

Chocolate-Nut Log Center:

1-1/2 cups (9 oz.) semisweet chocolate **pieces**	**1/2 cup sweetened condensed milk** **1-1/2 teaspoons vanilla extract**
2 tablespoons butter or margarine	**1-1/2 cups chopped walnuts**

Prepare Chocolate-Nut Log Center. Refrigerate Chocolate-Nut Log mixture until firm, at least 30 minutes. Divide mixture into 2 equal portions. On waxed paper, shape each portion into a log 12 inches long and 1 inch in diameter. Wrap and refrigerate until firm, at least 1 hour. Cover and refrigerate Basic Butter-Cookie Dough at least 30 minutes. Divide dough into 2 equal portions. Between 2 sheets of waxed paper, roll 1 portion into a 12-1/2" x 5" rectangle. Remove top sheet of waxed paper. Place a Chocolate-Nut Log Center in center of dough rectangle. Carefully bring dough up around filling, using sheet of waxed paper to help lift dough, covering filling completely and overlapping edges slightly. Smooth dough around filling, sealing edges and ends. Repeat with remaining dough and log center. Wrap and refrigerate until firm, several hours or overnight. To bake cookies, preheat oven to 375F (190C). Cut chilled dough into 1/4-inch slices. Place 1 inch apart on ungreased baking sheets. Bake 10 to 12 minutes or until edges are light golden. Cool 2 to 3 minutes on baking sheets; then remove to racks to cool completely. Makes about 90 (2-1/4-inch) cookies.

Chocolate-Nut Log Center:
In top of a double boiler, combine chocolate pieces and butter or margarine. Heat over hot but not boiling water until melted and smooth, stirring occasionally. Remove from heat. Stir in sweetened condensed milk, vanilla and walnuts.

Santa's Whiskers   *Photo on pages 154 and 155*

Delicate holiday cookies rolled in coconut add color to the festivities.

1 cup butter or margarine, room temperature	**1/3 cup finely chopped red candied cherries**
3/4 cup sugar	**1/3 cup finely chopped green**
2 tablespoons milk	**candied cherries**
1 teaspoon vanilla extract	**1/2 cup finely chopped walnuts**
2-1/2 cups all-purpose flour	**2/3 cup flaked or shredded coconut**

Preheat oven to 375F (190C). In a large bowl, beat together butter or margarine, sugar, milk and vanilla until light and fluffy. Add flour, beating well. Stir in candied cherries and nuts. Divide dough into 2 equal portions. Shape each portion into a log 8 inches long and 2 inches in diameter. Roll each log in 1/3 cup coconut, covering completely. Wrap and refrigerate until firm, several hours or overnight. To bake cookies, preheat oven to 375F (190C). Cut chilled dough into 1/4-inch slices. Place 1-1/2 inches apart on ungreased baking sheets. Bake 8 to 10 minutes or until edges are golden. Remove cookies from baking sheets; cool on racks. Makes about 62 (2-1/4-inch) cookies.

How to Make Two-Tone Cookie Roll

1/Place a chocolate log in center of dough. Bring dough around filling, using waxed paper to lift dough.

2/Cut dough into 1/4-inch slices. Place 1 inch apart on ungreased baking sheets.

Peanut-Butter-Oatmeal Slices

Very nutritious and tasty with whole-wheat flour and rolled oats.

1/4 cup butter or margarine,
   room temperature
1/4 cup vegetable shortening
1/2 cup smooth or crunchy peanut butter
1 cup packed brown sugar
1 teaspoon vanilla extract

1 egg
1-1/4 cups whole-wheat flour
1 teaspoon baking powder
Pinch of salt
1 cup rolled oats

In a large bowl, beat together butter or margarine, shortening, peanut butter, brown sugar, vanilla and egg until light and fluffy. Add flour, baking powder and salt, beating until well blended. Stir in oats. Divide dough into 2 equal portions. Shape each portion into a log 6 inches long and 1-3/4 inches in diameter. Wrap and freeze until firm, 1 to 2 hours. To bake cookies, preheat oven to 350F (175C). Lightly grease baking sheets. Cut frozen dough into 1/4-inch slices. Place 1-1/2 inches apart on greased baking sheets. Bake 12 to 14 minutes or until golden. Remove cookies from baking sheets; cool on racks. Makes about 46 (2-1/4-inch) cookies.

Viennese Almond-Apricot Wheels

Although time-consuming to make, these elegant cookies are worth the effort.

1/2 cup butter, room temperature
6 tablespoons sugar
1-1/2 teaspoons vanilla extract
1 cup all-purpose flour

1 cup finely ground blanched almonds
About 1/4 cup apricot jam
Chocolate Glaze, see below

Chocolate Glaze:
1/2 cup (3 oz.) semisweet chocolate pieces
1 tablespoon butter

1 tablespoon milk
1-1/2 teaspoons light corn syrup

In a medium bowl, beat together butter, sugar and vanilla until creamy. Add flour, beating until blended. Beat in almonds. Dough has a tendency to be dry. Press dough together with your fingers, if necessary. Shape dough into a log 7 inches long and 1-3/4 inches in diameter. Wrap and refrigerate until firm, several hours or overnight. To bake cookies, preheat oven to 350F (175C). Cut chilled dough into 1/8- to 3/16-inch slices. Place 1 inch apart on ungreased baking sheets. Bake 8 to 10 minutes or until cookies are barely golden. Remove cookies from baking sheets; cool on racks. Spread bottoms of half the cooled cookies with about 1/2 teaspoon jam each to within 1/4 inch of edges. Top with remaining cookies, bottom side toward jam. Prepare Chocolate Glaze. Line baking sheets with waxed paper. Dip half of each filled cookie into Chocolate Glaze. Place on waxed-paper-lined baking sheets. Let stand until set. Store in refrigerator. Makes about 20 (2-1/4-inch) filled cookies.

Chocolate Glaze:
In top of a double boiler, combine chocolate pieces and butter. Heat over hot but not boiling water until melted and smooth, stirring frequently. Or, in a 1-cup glass measure, heat together chocolate and butter in microwave oven on full power (HIGH) 1 to 1-1/2 minutes or until melted and smooth, stirring once. Remove from heat or microwave oven. Stir in milk and corn syrup until thoroughly blended.

Spicy Refrigerator Slices

These slice best when frozen.

1 cup butter or margarine, room temperature
1 cup sugar
2 eggs
1 teaspoon vanilla extract
3-1/2 cups all-purpose flour
1-1/2 teaspoons baking soda

1-1/2 teaspoons ground cinnamon
1/2 teaspoon ground nutmeg
1/4 teaspoon ground cloves
1 cup currants or chopped raisins
Sugar

In a large bowl, beat together butter or margarine, 1 cup sugar, eggs and vanilla until light and fluffy. Add flour, baking soda and spices, beating until blended. Stir in currants or raisins. Divide dough into 2 equal portions. Shape each portion into a rectangle 9-1/2 inches long, 2-1/4 inches wide and 1-1/2 inches thick. Wrap and freeze until firm, at least 1 hour. To bake cookies, preheat oven to 375F (190C). Cut frozen dough into 1/4-inch slices. Place 1 inch apart on ungreased baking sheets. Sprinkle with sugar. Bake 10 to 12 minutes or until golden. Remove cookies from baking sheets; cool on racks. Makes about 70 (2-3/4" x 2") cookies.

Back to front: Raspberry Swirls, page 48; Spicy Refrigerator Slices, above; and Viennese Almond-Apricot Wheels, above.

Rainbow Slices

One dough, flavored and colored differently, makes these pretty triple-layered cookies.

1 cup butter or margarine, room temperature
3/4 cup sugar
1 egg
1 teaspoon vanilla extract
2-1/2 cups all-purpose flour
1 teaspoon baking powder
Pinch of salt
4 drops red food coloring

1/4 cup finely chopped red candied cherries
2 oz. semisweet chocolate or
   1/3 cup (2 oz.) semisweet chocolate
   pieces, melted
1/3 cup finely chopped walnuts
1/2 teaspoon rum extract
1/3 cup flaked or shredded coconut

Line an 8'' x 4'' loaf pan with waxed paper or foil. In a large bowl, beat together butter or margarine, sugar, egg and vanilla until light and fluffy. Add flour, baking powder and salt, beating until blended. Divide dough into 3 equal portions. To 1 portion, blend in red food coloring. Then add candied cherries. To another portion, add melted chocolate and walnuts. To remaining portion, blend in rum extract. Then add coconut. Press pink dough in an even layer in bottom of lined pan. Cover evenly with chocolate dough. Top evenly with white dough. Cover and refrigerate until firm, several hours or overnight. To bake cookies, preheat oven to 350F (175C). Invert pan of chilled dough on a board; peel off waxed paper or foil. Cut into 1/4-inch crosswise slices. Cut each slice into 3 equal pieces. Place 1 inch apart on ungreased baking sheets. Bake 10 to 12 minutes or until edges are golden brown. Remove cookies from baking sheets; cool on racks. Makes about 84 (2'' x 1-1/4'') cookies.

Cheese Wafers   *Photo on pages 154 and 155*

For something savory alongside the sweet, try these tasty cheese cookies.

1/2 cup butter or margarine,
   room temperature
1-1/2 cups shredded Cheddar cheese
   (6 oz.)

Pinch of red (cayenne) pepper
1 cup all-purpose flour
2 tablespoons toasted sesame seeds
38 pecan halves, if desired

In a medium bowl, beat together butter or margarine, cheese and red pepper until thoroughly blended. Add flour, beating until blended. Shape dough into a log 9-1/2 inches long and 1-1/2 inches in diameter. Roll log in sesame seeds, coating completely. Wrap and refrigerate until firm, several hours or overnight. To bake cookies, preheat oven to 350F (175C). Cut chilled dough into 1/4-inch slices. Place 1 inch apart on ungreased baking sheets. Press a pecan half in center of each, if desired. Bake 12 to 14 minutes or until edges and bottoms are golden. Remove cookies from baking sheets; cool on racks. Makes about 38 (1-3/4-inch) cookies.

Tip

To toast sesame seeds, place in a shallow baking pan. Bake at 350F (175C) 10 to 12 minutes or until golden, stirring twice.

How to Make Rainbow Slices

1/Divide dough into 3 equal portions. Flavor and color dough as directed in recipe.

2/Layer dough in lined pan, pressing pink dough on bottom, adding chocolate dough and white dough.

3/Turn out chilled dough onto a board. Peel off paper or foil. Cut into 1/4-inch crosswise slices.

4/Cut each slice into 3 equal pieces. Place cookies 1 inch apart on ungreased baking sheets.

Rolled, Cut & Molded Cookies

Rolled, cut and molded cookies offer many opportunities for creativity and originality. You can cut, shape, press or decorate them in unlimited ways. However, they do require patience, time and loving care.

Before beginning to bake, read your selected recipe. Some doughs require chilling prior to rolling, cutting or shaping. When using dough that has been prepared several hours before baking, it may be necessary to allow the dough to stand at room temperature until pliable.

When holiday time is just around the corner, get out your cookie press. Make Mrs. Arnold's Spritz Cookies, a treasured recipe our family has been making for many years. Unlike many spritz doughs, this one is full of ground walnuts.

Hailing from Scandinavia are popular Danish Butter Cookies. Make them extra special by piping and shaping with a pastry bag fitted with a star decorating tube.

Adaptations of other ethnic specialties also enjoy a place in this collection. German favorites include Pfeffernüsse, Springerle and Lebkuchen. From the French we've borrowed Ladyfingers and Madeleines. Chinese Almond Cookies and Scottish Shortbread are at home here also.

Pretzel fanciers will delight in Black & White Pretzel Twists. With their cocoa-enhanced dough and white-chocolate topping, they are bound to be a hit. And they're easier to shape than you might imagine.

Cutout-cookie doughs come in a variety of flavors. When an indestructible dough is desired, turn to the All-Occasion Cutout Cookies. This recipe is the one to rely upon when working with the scout troop, having a cookie party or when the gang wants to get into the act. More delicate and fragile are Powdered-Sugar Cutouts, Old-Fashioned Sugar Cookies and Cream-Cheese Sugar Cookies.

When making rolled or cutout cookies, be stingy with flour. Reroll dough as seldom as possible to avoid tough cookies. For ease, work with only a portion of the dough at a time, keeping the remainder refrigerated. Cut cookies as close together as possible.

Use cookie cutters, cut shapes freehand with a pastry wheel or knife, or use cardboard-pattern inspirations you've traced or designed.

Bake and decorate cutout cookies for any occasion throughout the year. Just alter the cookie-cutter designs according to the season.

Black & White Pretzel Twists

The end result is worth the time and patience.

1 cup butter or margarine, room temperature
3/4 cup sugar
1 egg
1-1/2 teaspoons vanilla extract

1/2 cup unsweetened cocoa
2-1/2 cups all-purpose flour
8 oz. white chocolate, melted

Preheat oven to 325F (165C). In a large bowl, beat together butter or margarine, sugar, egg and vanilla until light and fluffy. Add cocoa and flour, beating until blended. Divide dough into 2 equal portions. Cut each portion into 24 equal pieces. On a piece of waxed paper, roll each piece of dough with your finger tips into a 7-inch-long rope. Twist into pretzel shape, 1-1/2 inches apart, on ungreased baking sheets. Bake 9 to 11 minutes or until bottoms start to brown. Do not overbake or cookies will be dry. Remove cookies from baking sheets; cool on racks. Dip top side of cooled cookies in melted white chocolate; dry on racks. Makes 48 (2-1/4" x 1-3/4") cookies.

Chocolate Whirligigs

A modern version of the chocolate-vanilla pinwheels you knew as a child.

1/2 cup butter or margarine,
   room temperature
1/2 cup sugar
1 egg yolk
1 teaspoon vanilla extract

Pinch of salt
3 tablespoons milk
1-1/2 cups all-purpose flour
1/2 teaspoon baking powder
1 oz. unsweetened chocolate, melted

In a medium bowl, beat together butter or margarine, sugar, egg yolk, vanilla and salt until light and fluffy. Beat in milk. Add flour and baking powder, beating until blended. Divide dough into 2 equal portions. To 1 portion add melted chocolate, blending well. Leave other portion plain. Wrap and refrigerate until firm enough to roll, 2 hours or longer. Dough will still be soft. On floured waxed paper, roll each portion into an 11" x 9" rectangle. Place white-dough rectangle on top of chocolate-dough rectangle, carefully peeling waxed paper from white dough. Roll up dough, jelly-roll fashion, from long side. Wrap and refrigerate until firm, several hours or overnight. To bake cookies, preheat oven to 375F (190C). Cut dough into 3/16-inch slices. Place 1 inch apart on ungreased baking sheets. Bake 8 to 10 minutes or until edges begin to turn golden. Remove cookies from baking sheets; cool on racks. Makes 50 to 55 (1-3/4-inch) cookies.

Variation

Peanut-Butter & Chocolate Whirligigs: Add 1/4 cup smooth peanut butter to 1 portion of plain dough. Add chocolate to other portion as above. Proceed as directed above.

Tip

When rolling out many dough strips the same size, cut a cardboard strip the length desired. Use it as a size guide. It's much simpler than measuring each one with a ruler or guessing.

How to Make All-Occasion Cutout Cookies

1/On a lightly floured surface, roll dough 1/4 inch thick. Do not overwork dough.

2/Cut dough into desired shapes. Place 1 inch apart on ungreased baking sheets.

3/Frost baked cookies as desired using Vanilla- or Chocolate-Buttercream Icing.

4/Decorate cookies using assorted candy pieces and colored icing forced through a pastry bag.

All-Occasion Cutout Cookies

A basic sugar-cookie dough that is almost indestructible. Great for a children's cookie party.

**1/2 cup butter or margarine,
    room temperature**
1 cup sugar
1 egg
2 to 3 tablespoons milk
1-1/2 teaspoons vanilla extract

2 to 2-1/4 cups all-purpose flour
2 teaspoons baking powder
1/4 teaspoon salt
Vanilla-Buttercream Icing, page 153
**Assorted decorations such as candies,
    raisins or colored sugar crystals**

In a medium bowl, beat together butter or margarine, sugar, egg, milk and vanilla until light and fluffy. Add flour, baking powder and salt, beating until blended. Divide dough into 2 equal portions. Wrap and refrigerate until firm, 1 hour or longer. Prior to baking, allow dough to stand at room temperature until soft enough to roll easily. To bake cookies, preheat oven to 375F (190C). On a lightly floured surface, roll dough 1/4 inch thick. With lightly floured cookie cutters, cut into desired shapes. Place 1 inch apart on ungreased baking sheets. Bake 7 to 10 minutes or until edges are golden. Remove cookies from baking sheets; cool on racks. Decorate as desired with Vanilla-Buttercream Icing and decorations. Let stand until set. Makes about 48 (2-1/2-inch) cookies.

Old-Fashioned Sugar Cookies

Light and fragile—fragrant and delicious.

1 cup butter, room temperature
1-1/2 cups granulated sugar
1 teaspoon vanilla extract
1 teaspoon orange extract
3 eggs

3-3/4 cups all-purpose flour
Pinch of salt
2 teaspoons baking powder
3/4 teaspoon baking soda
Red or green sugar crystals, if desired

In a large bowl, beat together butter, granulated sugar, vanilla, orange extract and eggs until light and fluffy. Beat in flour, salt, baking powder and baking soda until thoroughly blended. Divide dough into 2 equal portions. Wrap and refrigerate until firm, several hours or overnight. To bake cookies, preheat oven to 350F (175C). Grease baking sheets. On a floured surface, roll dough 3/16 to 1/4 inch thick. With lightly floured cookie cutters, cut into desired shapes. Place 1-1/2 inches apart on greased baking sheets. Sprinkle with red or green sugar, if desired. Bake 7 to 9 minutes or until pale in color. Baking time will depend on size and thickness of cookies. Watch carefully. Remove cookies from baking sheets; cool on racks. Makes about 80 (2-1/2-inch) cookies.

Tip

The yield of cutout-cookie recipes depends on the thickness of the rolled-out dough as well as the size and shape of the cookie cutters being used.

Cream-Cheese Sugar Cookies

If cream cheese is your pleasure, try this sugar-cookie variation.

1 cup butter or margarine, room temperature
1 (3-oz.) pkg. cream cheese,
  room temperature
3/4 cup granulated sugar
1 egg

Pinch of salt
2 teaspoons vanilla extract
1/2 teaspoon almond extract, if desired
3 cups all-purpose flour
Red or green sugar crystals, if desired

In a large bowl, beat together butter or margarine, cream cheese, granulated sugar, egg, salt, vanilla and almond extract, if desired, until light and fluffy. Add flour, beating until well blended. Divide dough into 2 equal portions. Wrap and refrigerate until firm, several hours or overnight. Prior to baking, allow dough to stand at room temperature until soft enough to roll easily. To bake cookies, preheat oven to 375F (190C). On a floured surface, roll dough 3/16 to 1/4 inch thick. With lightly floured cookie cutters, cut into desired shapes. Place 1 inch apart on ungreased baking sheets. Sprinkle with red or green sugar, if desired. Bake 7 to 10 minutes or until edges are golden. Remove cookies from baking sheets; cool on racks. Frost and decorate as desired. Makes about 45 (3-inch) cookies.

Powdered-Sugar Cutouts

Using paint brushes, decorate these tender cookies with Egg-Yolk Paint before baking.

1 cup butter or margarine, room temperature
1-1/2 cups powdered sugar
1 egg
1-1/2 teaspoons vanilla extract

2 tablespoons grated orange or lemon peel
2-1/4 cups all-purpose flour
1 teaspoon baking powder
Egg-Yolk Paint, see below

Egg-Yolk Paint:
1 egg yolk
1/4 to 1/2 teaspoon water

Assorted food colorings

In a medium bowl, beat together butter or margarine, powdered sugar, egg, vanilla and orange or lemon peel until light and fluffy. Add flour and baking powder, beating until blended. Wrap and refrigerate 2 to 3 hours. To bake cookies, preheat oven to 375F (190C). On a lightly floured surface, roll dough 3/16 to 1/4 inch thick. With lightly floured cookie cutters, cut dough into desired shapes. Place 1-1/2 inches apart on ungreased baking sheets. Prepare Egg-Yolk Paint. Using small paint brushes, paint designs on cookies, as desired, using Egg-Yolk Paint. Bake 8 to 10 minutes or until beginning to brown slightly around edges. Remove cookies from baking sheets; cool on racks. Makes about 40 (2-1/2-inch) cookies.

Egg-Yolk Paint:
In a small cup, combine egg yolk and water. Divide mixture among 3 or 4 custard cups. Tint each a different color.

This is a good cookie to cutout and use for place cards. Omit decorating cookies with Egg-Yolk Paint. After baking, pipe cookies with guests' names using Vanilla-Buttercream Icing, page 153, tinting colors as desired.

Potato-Chip Cookies

Don't add salt to this dough—potato chips provide salt along with crunchiness.

1/2 cup butter or margarine, room temperature	1/3 cup crushed potato chips
1/3 cup granulated sugar	1/3 cup chopped walnuts or pecans
3/4 teaspoon vanilla extract	1 tablespoon granulated sugar
1 cup all-purpose flour	Powdered sugar

Preheat oven to 350F (175C). In a medium bowl, beat together butter or margarine, 1/3 cup granulated sugar and vanilla until light and fluffy. Add flour, beating until blended. Stir in potato chips and nuts. Shape into 1-inch balls. Place 3 inches apart on ungreased baking sheets. Flatten cookies with bottom of a glass dipped in 1 tablespoon granulated sugar. Bake 12 to 15 minutes or until edges are lightly browned. Remove cookies from baking sheets; cool on racks. While slightly warm, sift powdered sugar over tops. Makes 32 to 34 (2-inch) cookies.

Festive Logs

Rich butter logs coated on one end with chocolate.

1 cup butter or margarine, room temperature	2 cups all-purpose flour
1/3 cup granulated sugar	2 cups chopped pecans
2 teaspoons brandy	Sifted powdered sugar
2 teaspoons vanilla extract	1/2 cup (3 oz.) semisweet chocolate pieces,
1/4 teaspoon salt	melted

Preheat oven to 325F (165C). In a large bowl, beat together butter or margarine and granulated sugar until light and fluffy. Beat in brandy, vanilla and salt. Add flour, beating until blended. Stir in pecans. Shape dough into small logs, each 2-1/2 inches long and 1/2 inch wide. Place 2 inches apart on ungreased baking sheets. Bake 15 to 20 minutes. Cookies should not brown. Remove cookies from baking sheets; cool on racks. While still slightly warm, roll in powdered sugar. Dip 1 end of each cooled cookie in melted chocolate. Let stand until set. Makes about 48 (2-1/2" x 1/2") cookies.

Cornmeal-Butter Wafers

Tender, buttery and crisp, cornmeal adds crunch and nut-like flavor.

1 cup butter or margarine, room temperature	2 teaspoons grated orange peel
1 cup sugar	1 cup yellow cornmeal
2 egg yolks	1-1/2 cups all-purpose flour

In a large bowl, beat together butter or margarine, sugar, egg yolks and orange peel until light and fluffy. Add cornmeal and flour, beating until blended. Cover and refrigerate until firm, about 1 hour. To bake cookies, preheat oven to 350F (175C). Lightly grease baking sheets. On a floured surface, roll dough 1/4 inch thick. With lightly floured 2-1/2-inch cookie cutters, cut into desired shapes. Place 1 inch apart on greased baking sheets. Bake 10 to 12 minutes or until edges are golden. Cool 2 to 3 minutes on baking sheets; then remove to racks to cool completely. Makes about 48 (2-1/2-inch) cookies.

How to Make Danish Butter Cookies

1/Place dough in a large pastry bag fitted with a large open-star 3/4-inch-diameter decorating tube, filling bag half-full at a time.

2/Pipe dough into 1-1/2-inch diameter cookies on ungreased baking sheets. Top each cookie with a cherry half, pressing in lightly.

Danish Butter Cookies

On a sojourn to Denmark, this delicious recipe was shared by a Danish home economist.

1 cup butter, room temperature
1 cup sugar
1 egg

2 cups all-purpose flour
30 whole red or green candied cherries,
    cut in halves

Preheat oven to 375F (190C). In a medium bowl, beat together butter, sugar and egg until light and fluffy. Add flour, beating until blended. Place dough in a large pastry bag fitted with a large open-star 3/4-inch-diameter decorating tube, filling bag half-full at a time. Pipe dough into 1-1/2-inch-diameter cookies, 2 inches apart, on ungreased baking sheets. Top center of each cookie with a cherry half, pressing in lightly. Bake 8 to 10 minutes or until edges are golden. Cookies should not brown on top. Remove cookies from baking sheets; cool on racks. Makes about 60 (2-inch) cookies.

Variation

Butter Refrigerator Cookies: Add 1 teaspoon vanilla extract to butter-egg mixture. After adding flour, stir in 1/2 cup chopped blanched almonds. Divide dough into 2 equal portions. Shape each portion into a log 7 inches long and 1-3/4 inches in diameter. Wrap and refrigerate until firm, several hours or overnight. To bake cookies, preheat oven to 350F (175C). Cut logs into 1/4-inch slices. Place 2 inches apart on ungreased baking sheets. Bake 9 to 11 minutes or until edges are golden. Remove cookies from baking sheets; cool on racks. Makes 55 to 60 (2-1/4-inch) cookies.

Hazelnut Macaroons

Chewy with the flavor of hazelnuts—a good choice to serve with ice cream.

2 egg whites
1/2 cup packed brown sugar
1 teaspoon vanilla extract

1 tablespoon all-purpose flour
1-3/4 cups finely ground hazelnuts

Preheat oven to 350F (175C). Line baking sheets with foil. In a medium bowl, beat egg whites with electric mixer until foamy. Gradually add brown sugar, continuing to beat at high speed until shiny and stiff peaks form. Beat in vanilla and flour until thoroughly blended. Fold in hazelnuts. Using a spatula, place batter in a large pastry bag fitted with a large round 1/2-inch-diameter decorating tube, filling bag half-full at a time. Pipe batter into 1-1/2-inch cookies, 1 inch apart, on foil-lined baking sheets. Bake 11 to 13 minutes or until golden brown. Remove cookies from baking sheets; cool on racks. Makes 25 to 30 (1-3/4-inch) cookies.

Chocolate-Peppermint Bites

Serve in place of after-dinner mints.

3/4 teaspoon peppermint extract
1/2 recipe Basic Butter-Cookie Dough,
   page 117

1/2 cup (3 oz.) miniature semisweet
   chocolate pieces
1/2 recipe Chocolate Glaze, page 53

Preheat oven to 350F (175C). Add 1/2 teaspoon peppermint extract to Basic Butter-Cookie Dough, blending well. Stir in chocolate pieces. Shape dough into 1-inch balls. Place 1-1/2 inches apart on ungreased baking sheets. Bake 10 to 12 minutes or until bottoms are golden. Remove cookies from baking sheets; cool on racks. Meanwhile, prepare Chocolate Glaze, adding remaining 1/4 teaspoon peppermint extract. Dip tops of cooled cookies in Chocolate Glaze. Let stand until set. Makes 32 to 34 (1-1/2-inch) cookies.

Chinese Almond Cookies

Lard makes the difference in these Chinese specialties.

1 cup (8 oz.) lard, room temperature
1 egg
3/4 teaspoon almond extract
1/2 cup granulated sugar
1/2 cup packed brown sugar

2-1/4 cups all-purpose flour
1-1/4 teaspoons baking powder
50 to 55 whole blanched almonds
1 egg yolk, beaten

Preheat oven to 350F (175C). In a medium bowl, beat together lard, 1 egg, almond extract, granulated sugar and brown sugar until creamy. Add flour and baking powder, beating until well blended. Shape dough into 1-1/4-inch balls. Place 2 inches apart on ungreased baking sheets. Press an almond in the center of each. Brush cookies with beaten egg yolk. Bake 14 to 15 minutes or until golden. Watch carefully. Remove cookies from baking sheets; cool on racks. Makes 50 to 55 (2-inch) cookies.

Festive Raisin Pillows

Nifty little pastry pillows filled with a piquant raisin mixture and topped with icing.

1-3/4 cups raisins	1 egg
3/4 cup granulated suqar	2 tablespoons lemon juice
3 tablespoons all-purpose flour	1 cup chopped walnuts
Pinch of salt	2 sticks pie-crust mix
1/3 cup water	Icing, see below

Icing:

1 teaspoon butter or margarine, melted	1-1/2 cups sifted powdered sugar
1 tablespoon warm water	Red food coloring, if desired
1/2 teaspoon vanilla extract	

In a medium saucepan, combine raisins, granulated sugar, flour and salt. Stir in water and egg. Cook over medium heat until thick, 5 to 6 minutes, stirring constantly. Stir in lemon juice and walnuts. Cool. Preheat oven to 425F (220C). Prepare pie-crust mix according to package directions. Divide dough into 2 equal portions. Roll each portion into a 9-inch square. Place 1 square on an ungreased baking sheet; spread evenly with cooled raisin mixture. Cover with remaining pie-crust square. With a sharp knife, cut into 25 pastry squares but do not separate. Bake 25 to 30 minutes or until lightly browned. Cool on baking sheet. Meanwhile, prepare Icing. While slightly warm, spread cookies with Icing. Let stand until set. Cut cooled cookies into squares as marked. Makes 25 (1-3/4-inch) cookies.

Icing:

In a small bowl, combine melted butter or margarine, warm water, vanilla and powdered sugar, stirring until smooth. Tint with a few drops of red food coloring, if desired.

Date-Nut Fancies

Whip up this cream-cheese dough in a food processor; then wrap it around a nut-stuffed date.

1 (8-oz.) pkg. cream cheese, room temperature	2 cups all-purpose flour
1 cup butter, room temperature	64 whole dates or prunes, pitted
1 cup sugar	64 pecan halves or whole blanched almonds
2 teaspoons vanilla extract	Powdered sugar

In a food processor fitted with a steel blade, process cream cheese, butter, sugar and vanilla until smooth. Add flour; process until well blended and dough begins to cling together in a ball. Refrigerate dough until firm, about 1 hour. To bake cookies, preheat oven to 350F (175C). Stuff each date or prune with a nut, breaking nuts, if necessary, to fit in entire piece. Cut dough into 64 equal portions. Flatten each portion of dough in the palm of your hand. Wrap dough around a stuffed date or prune, enclosing completely. Pinch to seal. Place 1-1/2 inches apart on ungreased baking sheets. Bake 15 to 17 minutes or until beginning to color. Cool 2 to 3 minutes on baking sheets; then remove to racks to cool completely. While warm, sift powdered sugar over tops. Makes 64 (1-3/4-inch) cookies.

Peanutty Chocolate Crinkles

Peanut-butter and chocolate fans will take a shine to these crackle-top cookies.

1/2 cup butter or margarine, room temperature	2 teaspoons baking powder
1-1/2 cups granulated sugar	1/4 teaspoon salt
3 eggs	1/2 cup chopped walnuts
1 tablespoon vanilla extract	1/2 cup (3 oz.) semisweet chocolate pieces, if desired
3 oz. unsweetened chocolate, melted	1 cup (6 oz.) peanut-butter-flavor pieces
2 cups all-purpose flour	Sifted powdered sugar

In a large bowl, beat together butter or margarine, granulated sugar, eggs and vanilla until light and fluffy. Beat in melted unsweetened chocolate. Add flour, baking powder and salt, beating well. Stir in walnuts, chocolate pieces, if desired, and peanut-butter pieces. Cover and refrigerate 1 hour or longer. To bake cookies, preheat oven to 350F (175C). Grease baking sheets. Shape dough into 1-inch balls; roll in powdered sugar, coating well. Place 2 inches apart on greased baking sheets. Bake 10 minutes. Cookies will be soft. Do not overbake. Remove cookies from baking sheets; cool on racks. Makes 65 to 70 (1-1/2-inch) cookies.

Pecan-Shortbread Cookie Tarts

Bake these buttery tarts in miniature fluted tins available in cookware shops.

1-1/4 cups all-purpose flour	1/2 teaspoon vanilla extract
1/2 cup butter, room temperature	1/4 cup finely chopped pecans
3 tablespoons sugar	

Preheat oven to 350F (175C). In a medium bowl, combine flour, butter, sugar, vanilla and pecans. Blend with a fork until mixture resembles fine crumbs. Knead until dough holds together. Press a scant tablespoon of dough into bottom and up sides of each of 25 ungreased 2- to 2-1/2-inch miniature fluted tart pans. Place tart pans 1-inch apart on baking sheets. Bake 10 to 11 minutes or until lightly golden. Cool slightly in pans; then with the point of a sharp knife loosen edges to release tarts from pans. Cool on racks. Serve plain, upside down, or fill each with raspberry jam or serve with a bowl of whipped cream mixed with a little of your favorite jam preserves. Makes about 25 (2- to 2-1/2-inch) cookie tarts.

Variation

Cream-Cheese-Filled Cookie Tarts: Just before serving, spread cooled baked cookie tarts with a little Cream-Cheese Filling and top with a dab of warmed raspberry jam or a fresh strawberry slice or kiwi slice. To make Cream-Cheese Filling, in a small bowl, beat together 1 (3-ounce) package room-temperature cream cheese, 1 tablespoon whipping cream or milk, 2 tablespoons powdered sugar and 1/2 teaspoon vanilla extract until smooth.

Tip

When rolling cookie dough on a floured surface, there are several options. Roll it on a marble slab, waxed paper, pastry cloth or right on the baking sheet.

Mrs. Arnold's Spritz Cookies   *Photo on pages 154 and 155*

A holiday tradition in our family since the '40s when a friend shared it with us.

2 cups butter, room temperature
2 cups granulated sugar
1 tablespoon vanilla extract
4 eggs
2 cups finely chopped or ground walnuts
6 cups all-purpose flour
1 teaspoon baking powder

10 red candied cherries, each cut in
   10 pieces
20 green candied cherries, each cut in
   10 lengthwise slivers
Red or green sugar crystals
Silver dragées

In an extra-large bowl, use an electric mixer to beat together butter, granulated sugar, vanilla and eggs until fluffy. Gradually beat in walnuts, flour and baking powder, blending thoroughly. Divide dough into 2 portions. Use dough immediately or wrap and refrigerate up to 3 days. If dough has been chilled, let stand at room temperature until pliable enough to press through a cookie press. Use 1 portion of dough to make wreaths and the other portion to make Christmas trees, rosettes or stars. To bake cookies, preheat oven to 375F (190C). Fill a cookie press with dough. To make wreaths, fit cookie press with star disk. Force dough onto cold ungreased baking sheets in a continuous strip. Cut strips into 5-inch-long pieces. Shape each piece into a circle. Continue forming wreaths until baking sheet is filled, arranging them 1 inch apart. Form a bow on each wreath by centering a red-cherry piece between 2 slivers of green cherries. To make Christmas trees, rosettes or stars, fit cookie press with Christmas tree, rosette or star disk. For each, stand cookie press upright on cold ungreased baking sheet. Force dough out to form tree, rosette or star. Release pressure and lift up slightly to cut off dough. Cookies should be 1-1/2 inches apart. Sprinkle with red or green sugar and place silver dragées on each as desired. Bake 8 to 10 minutes or until bottoms are golden. Tops should be pale, not brown. Remove from baking sheets; cool on racks. Makes about 100 (2-inch) wreaths and 100 (2-inch) trees, rosettes or stars.

Variation

Chocolate Spritz: Add 1/4 cup unsweetened cocoa to 1/4 recipe of the dough, blending thoroughly. Bake at 375F (190C) 5 to 7 minutes or until bottoms are lightly browned.

Scandinavian Bird's Nests

A jam-topped cookie that's been part of my mother's holiday repertoire for many years.

1/2 cup butter or margarine,
   room temperature
1/4 cup packed brown sugar
1 egg, separated

1 cup all-purpose flour
1/2 cup finely chopped walnuts
3 tablespoons currant jelly or raspberry jam

Preheat oven to 350F (175C). Grease baking sheets. In a medium bowl, beat together butter or margarine, brown sugar and egg yolk until light and fluffy. Add flour, beating until blended. Shape into 1-inch balls. In a small bowl, beat egg white slightly. Dip balls into egg white, then in walnuts, coating completely. Place 1-1/2 inches apart on greased baking sheets. With the end of a wooden-spoon handle, make a deep depression in center of each cookie, being careful not to go all the way to bottom of dough. Bake 13 to 15 minutes or until cookies start to turn golden brown. Remove cookies from baking sheets; cool on racks. While warm, with the tip of a teaspoon, place a small amount of jelly or jam in depression in center of each cookie. Jelly or jam will not melt but will form a thin crust, if cookies are not too hot. Makes about 24 (1-1/2-inch) cookies.

How to Make Mrs. Arnold's Spritz Cookies

1/Fill a cookie press with dough. To make wreaths, fit press with a star disk. Force dough onto cold ungreased baking sheets in a continuous strip.

2/Cut dough strips into 5-inch-long pieces. Shape each piece into a circle. Garnish each wreath with a red-cherry piece and 2 slivers of a green cherry.

Fancy Lace Turtles

Elegant crisp lacy base flavored with pecans and rum.

1/4 cup butter	2 teaspoons rum extract
1/4 cup packed brown sugar	104 pecan halves (about 2 cups)
3 tablespoons light corn syrup	1-1/2 cups (9 oz.) semisweet chocolate
1/3 cup all-purpose flour	pieces or chocolate-coating wafers,
3/4 cup finely chopped pecans	melted

Preheat oven to 350F (175C). Line baking sheets with foil. **Do not grease.** Use a new piece of foil for each baking sheet of cookies. In a medium saucepan, combine butter, brown sugar and corn syrup. Cook over medium heat until butter melts and mixture boils, stirring constantly. Remove from heat. All at once, stir in flour, chopped pecans and rum extract until thoroughly blended. Drop by heaping half-teaspoonfuls, 2-1/2 inches apart, on foil-lined baking sheets. Top each small bit of dough with 2 pecan halves, pressing into dough to secure. Pecan halves will completely cover dough, but dough spreads out during baking. Bake 8 to 9 minutes or until a rich golden color. Cool on foil. Carefully peel foil from cooled cookies. Top each cooled cookie with a dollop of melted chocolate. Let stand until set. Makes about 52 (2-1/2-inch) cookies.

Springerle

These anise-scented German cookies must dry overnight before baking.

4 eggs
2-1/4 cups powdered sugar
1-1/2 tablespoons anise extract or
   2 to 3 drops anise oil
2 teaspoons grated lemon peel

4-1/2 cups sifted cake flour
1 teaspoon baking powder
1/3 cup anise seeds
2 tablespoons all-purpose flour
2 tablespoons powdered sugar

In a large bowl, beat eggs and 2-1/4 cups powdered sugar with electric mixer at high speed until thick and light-colored, about 10 minutes. Add anise extract or oil and lemon peel. Gradually add cake flour and baking powder, beating until blended. Cover and refrigerate several hours or overnight. Grease 2 baking sheets. Sprinkle each with half the anise seeds. On a floured surface, knead dough 3 to 4 minutes; then roll 1/4 inch thick. In a small bowl, combine all-purpose flour and 2 tablespoons powdered sugar. Dust wooden springerle molds or springerle rolling pin with flour-sugar mixture, removing excess. Press or roll molds firmly into dough to make clear designs. Cut cookies apart, if necessary. Trim edges. Place cookies 1-1/2 inches apart, design-side up, on greased and seed-sprinkled baking sheets. Cover with tea towels; allow to dry at room temperature 12 to 24 hours to set design. To bake cookies, preheat oven to 250F (120C). Remove tea towels from cookies. Bake 40 minutes or until bottoms are golden. Tops should be white. Remove cookies from baking sheets; cool on racks. Store in an airtight container 1 to 2 weeks. Put a slice of apple in the container to help soften the cookies. It will take a few days, but check daily to make sure apple doesn't mold. Makes about 20 (3-3/4" x 2-1/2") cookies or many more if you use smaller molds.

Madeleines

Traditional French sponge-cake-like cookies baked in special shell-shaped molds.

2 eggs
1/3 cup sugar
1/2 teaspoon vanilla extract
1 teaspoon grated orange peel or lemon peel

3/4 cup sifted all-purpose flour
1/3 cup unsalted butter, melted, cooled
Sugar

Preheat oven to 375F (190C). Brush madeleine molds with soft, not melted, butter; dust molds with flour. In a medium bowl, beat together eggs, 1/3 cup sugar and vanilla with electric mixer at high speed until light-colored and tripled in volume, 10 to 15 minutes. Stir in orange or lemon peel. Gently fold in flour until blended. Fold in cooled butter. Spoon batter into buttered and floured madeleine molds, filling almost to top. Bake 10 to 12 minutes or until cookies spring back when touched with your finger tip. Remove cookies from molds; cool on racks. While warm, sprinkle with sugar. Makes 18 (3-inch) Madeleines.

Tip

Madeleine molds must be buttered and floured before adding each batch of batter.

Back to front: Springerle, above; Scottish Shortbread, page 74; and Madeleines, above.

Speculaas Cutouts

Crisp flat cinnamon-spiced cookies—traditional at holiday time in the low countries of northern Europe.

1/2 cup butter or margarine,
   room temperature
1 cup packed brown sugar
1 egg

1 teaspoon vanilla extract
2 cups all-purpose flour
1/2 teaspoon baking powder
1 tablespoon ground cinnamon

In a large bowl, beat together butter or margarine, brown sugar, egg and vanilla until light and fluffy. Add flour, baking powder and cinnamon, beating until blended. Wrap and refrigerate until firm, several hours or overnight. To bake cookies, preheat oven to 350F (175C). Grease baking sheets. On a floured surface, roll dough 3/16 to 1/4 inch thick. With floured cookie cutters, cut into desired shapes. Place 1/2 inch apart on greased baking sheets. Bake 6 to 8 minutes for 3/16-inch-thick cookies and 8 to 10 minutes for 1/4-inch-thick cookies or until edges begin to turn dark. Cool 2 to 3 minutes on baking sheets; then remove to racks to cool completely. Makes 20 to 36 (3-inch) cookies, depending on thickness of dough.

Ladyfingers

Pipe this very soft batter quickly, holding pastry bag almost horizontal to baking sheet.

3 eggs, separated
2 tablespoons granulated sugar
1 teaspoon vanilla extract

1/3 cup granulated sugar
3/4 cup sifted cake flour
Powdered sugar

Preheat oven to 325F (165C). Line baking sheets with foil. In a large bowl, beat egg whites with electric mixer at high speed until soft peaks form. Gradually add 2 tablespoons granulated sugar, beating until stiff peaks form; set aside. In a large bowl, beat egg yolks, vanilla and 1/3 cup granulated sugar with mixer at high speed until thick and light-colored, about 5 minutes. Gently fold in flour. Fold 1/3 of beaten egg whites into yolk mixture; then gently fold in remaining egg whites only until blended. Using a spatula, place batter in a large pastry bag fitted with a large round 1/2-inch-diameter decorating tube, filling bag half-full at a time. Pipe batter into strips, each 3-1/2 inches long and 1 inch wide, on foil-lined baking sheets. Cookies should be placed 1-1/2 inches apart. Sift powdered sugar over tops. Bake 10 to 12 minutes or until lightly colored. Do not brown. Remove cookies from baking sheets; cool on racks. Makes about 35 (3-1/2" x 1-1/4") Ladyfingers.

Tip

If cookies lose their crispness during storage, heat them in a 300F (150C) oven 3 to 5 minutes prior to serving.

Rugelach

Tasty little rolled cream-cheese cookies filled with nuts and chocolate or jam.

1 recipe Cream-Cheese Pastry, page 116
Nut Filling, see below

Powdered sugar, if desired

Nut Filling:
1/2 cup miniature semisweet chocolate pieces
  or currants
1 cup finely chopped walnuts

1/2 cup sugar
2-1/4 teaspoons ground cinnamon
1-1/2 tablespoons butter, melted

Cover and refrigerate Cream-Cheese Pastry several hours or overnight. Prepare Nut Filling; set aside. To bake cookies, preheat oven to 375F (190C). Divide dough into 3 equal portions. On a floured board, roll each portion into an 11- to 12-inch circle. Spread each circle evenly with 1/3 of Nut Filling. Cut each circle into 16 equal wedges. Roll up wedges, beginning from wide end, pressing tip to secure. Place point-side down on ungreased baking sheets. Bake 15 to 20 minutes or until golden. Remove cookies from baking sheets; cool on racks. While warm, sift powdered sugar over tops, if desired. Makes about 48 (1-1/2-inch) cookies.

Nut Filling:
In a medium bowl, combine chocolate pieces or currants, nuts, sugar, cinnamon and butter.

Variation
Jam-Filled Rugelach: Substitute Jam Filling for Nut Filling. To make Jam Filling, in a medium bowl, combine 1 cup finely chopped almonds or walnuts and 1/3 cup raspberry or apricot jam. Proceed as directed above.

Fattigmand

"Poor man's cakes" is the literal translation of these deep-fried Norwegian cookies.

Oil for deep-frying
2 egg yolks
2 tablespoons granulated sugar
2 tablespoons whipping cream

1/4 teaspoon ground mace
1/2 teaspoon brandy extract
3/4 to 1 cup all-purpose flour
Powdered sugar

In a small deep saucepan, pour oil to a 2- to 2-1/2-inch depth. Heat oil to 375F (190C) or until a 1-inch cube of bread turns golden brown in 50 seconds. In a medium bowl, beat together egg yolks and granulated sugar until light-colored. Stir in cream, mace and brandy extract. Beat in enough flour to make a dough firm enough to roll. Divide dough into 2 portions. Between sheets of waxed paper, roll dough 1/16 inch thick. With pastry wheel or fattigmand roller, cut dough into 4" x 2" diamonds. Make a lengthwise slit in center of each diamond; push long point of 1 end through slit and curl back. Fry, a few at a time, in hot oil, 35 to 40 seconds or until golden, turning once. Drain on paper towels; cool. Store airtight. Before serving, sift powdered sugar over both sides of cookies. Makes about 20 (2-1/2" x 2") cookies.

Lebkuchen

A spicy German tradition; this version was shared by a favorite aunt.

1 cup honey
1/2 cup molasses
1 cup packed brown sugar
1 egg
1 teaspoon grated lemon peel
1 tablespoon grated orange peel
4-1/2 cups all-purpose flour
1 cup finely chopped blanched almonds
1/2 teaspoon baking soda

1 tablespoon ground cinnamon
1-1/2 teaspoons ground cloves
1/4 teaspoon ground nutmeg
1/4 cup finely chopped candied orange peel
2 tablespoons finely chopped citron
Sugar Glaze, see below
Blanched-almond slices and
   red-candied-cherry pieces, if desired

Sugar Glaze:
3/4 cup granulated sugar
1/3 cup water

3 tablespoons powdered sugar

In a medium saucepan, bring honey, molasses and brown sugar to a boil, stirring occasionally. Remove from heat; cool until slighty warm. In a large bowl, beat together cooled honey mixture, egg, lemon peel and orange peel. Add flour, chopped almonds, baking soda, cinnamon, cloves and nutmeg, beating until blended. Stir in candied orange peel and citron until blended. Dough will be stiff, but sticky. Wrap and refrigerate several hours or overnight. To bake cookies, preheat oven to 350F (175C). Grease baking sheets. Divide dough into 2 equal portions. Work with 1 portion of dough at a time. On a floured surface, roll dough 1/4 inch thick. Using floured 2-1/2-inch cookie cutters, cut into hearts or rounds. Place cookies 1 inch apart on greased baking sheets. Bake 12 minutes or until done. Meanwhile, prepare Sugar Glaze; keep hot. Remove cookies from baking sheets; cool on racks. Brush hot cookies with hot Sugar Glaze. Decorate with almond slices and candied cherries, if desired. Allow cookies to dry. Store in an airtight container 1 to 2 weeks to age and soften. Put a slice of apple in the container to help soften the cookies. It will take a few days, but check daily to make sure apple doesn't mold. Makes about 50 (3-inch) hearts or rounds.

Sugar Syrup:

In a medium saucepan, combine granulated sugar and water. Bring to a boil; reduce heat and simmer 3 minutes. Remove from heat; stir in powdered sugar.

Variation

Lebkuchen Bars: Line 2 (15'' x 10'') jelly-roll pans with foil; grease foil. On well-floured waxed paper, roll each dough portion into a 15'' x 10'' rectangle. Invert dough on greased foil-lined pan. Peel off waxed paper. Score into 3'' x 2'' rectangles. Bake 20 to 25 minutes or until done. Cut along scored marks. Brush hot cookies with hot Sugar Glaze. Decorate with almond slices and candied cherries, if desired. Cool in pan 15 minutes; then remove to racks to cool completely. Makes 50 (3'' x 2'') cookies.

Tip *Avoid over-flouring the pastry cloth or board when rolling cookies. Excess flour may cause an unappealing crust on the bottom of the cookie.*

Pfeffernüsse

A classic German cookie, also known as "pepper nut."

2 eggs
1 cup sugar
2 cups all-purpose flour
1/2 teaspoon baking powder
1/4 teaspoon salt
1/4 teaspoon white or black pepper
1 teaspoon ground cinnamon

1/2 teaspoon ground cloves
1/2 teaspoon ground nutmeg
1 teaspoon grated lemon peel
1/4 cup finely chopped or
   ground blanched almonds
Honey Frosting, see below

Honey Frosting:
1 egg white
2 teaspoons honey

1/4 teaspoon ground anise seed
1-1/2 cups powdered sugar

Preheat oven to 350F (175C). Lightly grease baking sheets. In a large bowl, beat together eggs and sugar until light. Add flour, baking powder, salt, pepper, cinnamon, cloves, nutmeg and lemon peel, beating until well blended. Beat in almonds. Shape into 1-inch balls. Place 1-1/2 inches apart on greased baking sheets. Bake 13 to 15 minutes or until bottoms are lightly browned. Remove cookies from baking sheets; cool on racks. Prepare Honey Frosting. Place 10 to 12 cooled cookies in a small bowl. Add 2 tablespoons Honey Frosting. Stir to frost all sides of cookies. With a fork, lift out cookies; arrange on a rack to dry. Repeat until all cookies are frosted. Store cookies in an airtight container 1 week to ripen, if desired. Makes about 48 (1-1/4-inch) cookies.

Honey Frosting:
In a small bowl, combine egg white, honey and anise seed. Gradually add powdered sugar, beating until smooth.

Melting Moments   *Photo on pages 154 and 155*

Cornstarch is the ingredient that helps make these so tender.

1 cup butter or margarine, room temperature
1/2 cup powdered sugar
1/2 cup cornstarch

1-1/3 cups all-purpose flour
Red or green sugar crystals, if desired

In a medium bowl, beat together butter or margarine and powdered sugar until light and fluffy. Add cornstarch and flour, beating until blended. Cover and refrigerate 1 hour. To bake cookies, preheat oven to 325F (165C). Shape dough into 1-inch balls. Roll in colored sugar, if desired. Place 2 inches apart on ungreased baking sheets. Bake 12 to 15 minutes or until edges are golden. Cool 2 to 3 minutes on baking sheet; then remove to racks to cool completely. Makes about 45 (1-1/2-inch) cookies.

Variation
Before baking, roll balls in flaked or shredded coconut instead of sugar crystals. Dough may also be tinted with food coloring before rolling into balls.

Chocolate Shortbread

Chocoholics will appreciate this tender delicious variation.

1/2 cup butter, room temperature	1 cup (6 oz.) semisweet chocolate pieces,
1/4 cup packed brown sugar	melted
1/2 teaspoon vanilla extract	1 cup all-purpose flour

Preheat oven to 300F (150C). In a medium bowl, beat together butter, brown sugar and vanilla until light and fluffy. Beat in melted chocolate. Add flour, blending well. Press dough evenly into an ungreased 8- or 9-inch springform pan. Impress edge of dough with the tines of a fork. Prick surface evenly all over with fork tines. Bake 45 to 50 minutes or until set and almost firm to touch. While warm, cut into 10 wedges. Cool in pan. Makes 10 cookies.

Variation

Butterscotch Shortbread: Omit chocolate; proceed as directed above. Bake 40 to 45 minutes or until a pale golden brown.

Scottish Shortbread   *Photo on page 69.*

For an attractive look, bake in a stoneware shortbread mold.

1 cup butter, room temperature	1 teaspoon vanilla extract
1/4 cup powdered sugar	1/3 cup rice flour
1/4 cup granulated sugar	1-2/3 cups all-purpose flour

Preheat oven to 325F (165C). Brush a 10-inch stoneware shortbread mold or an 8- or 9-inch springform pan with melted butter. In a large bowl, beat together butter, powdered sugar, granulated sugar and vanilla until light and fluffy. Add rice flour and all-purpose flour. Using your hands, work mixture together until smooth and no longer crumbly. Do not overwork. Pat dough evenly into buttered mold or pan. Bake 35 to 45 minutes or until light golden and still somewhat springy to the touch. Cool 15 minutes in mold; then gently loosen shortbread by running knife around edge of mold. Invert mold on a plate and carefully lift mold from shortbread. If using a springform pan, do not invert; cool in pan on a rack. While slightly warm, cut shortbread into 8 wedges. Makes 8 cookies.

Cocoa-Coffee Bon Bons

A friend developed these delicious goodies to satisfy my chocolate craving.

2 cups creme-filled-chocolate-cookie crumbs	1/3 cup coffee-flavor liqueur
1/2 cup powdered sugar	1 cup chopped pecans
2 tablespoons unsweetened cocoa	3 tablespoons granulated sugar
2 tablespoons light corn syrup	6 oz. semisweet or white chocolate, melted

In a medium bowl, combine cookie crumbs, powdered sugar, cocoa, corn syrup, liqueur and pecans, blending well. Cover and refrigerate 1 hour or longer for ease in handling. Shape dough into 1-inch balls. Roll in granulated sugar. Store in airtight container for at least 1 day. Line a baking sheet with waxed paper. Dip half of each ball in melted chocolate; place 1/2 inch apart on waxed-paper-lined baking sheet. Refrigerate until firm. Store in refrigerator. Makes about 36 (1-inch) cookies.

How to Make Cookie Candy Canes

1/Shape 1 teaspoon of each color dough into a 4-inch-long rope, rolling back and forth on waxed paper to get smooth, even ropes.

2/Lightly press together a red-and-white rope; then twist together. Place on ungreased baking sheets. Curve 1 end down to form a candy cane or shape into hearts.

Cookie Candy Canes *Photo on pages 154 and 155*

Try forming twisted dough into other shapes such as hearts, alphabet letters or wreaths.

1 recipe Basic Butter-Cookie Dough, page 117 **1 egg white, beaten slightly**
1/2 teaspoon peppermint extract **Red sugar crystals**
3/4 teaspoon red food coloring

Preheat oven to 375F (190C). Prepare Basic Butter-Cookie Dough, adding peppermint extract along with vanilla. Divide dough into 2 equal portions. Stir red food coloring into 1 portion of dough, beating or kneading until well blended. For each cookie, shape 1 teaspoon of each color dough into a 4-inch-long rope, rolling back and forth on waxed paper to get smooth, even ropes. Place 1 red rope and 1 white rope side by side; press together lightly and twist. Place 1 inch apart on ungreased baking sheets. Curve 1 end of cookie down to form handle of candy cane. Brush with slightly beaten egg white and sprinkle with red sugar. Bake 8 to 10 minutes or until edges begin to brown lightly. Remove cookies from baking sheets; cool on racks. Makes about 46 (3-inch) cookies.

Variation

Valentine Hearts: On baking sheets, shape red-and-white twisted dough ropes into hearts, pressing together at point of heart where ends meet. Proceed as directed above.

Traditional Cookies

Just as trends in fashion come and go, so do trends in cookies. However, some of them have withstood the test of time, becoming favorites with each succeeding generation. This section is filled with those treasured keepsakes—longtime favorites we can't live without. All have been adapted and updated to utilize modern equipment and techniques without sacrificing flavor.

Who doesn't love America's most popular homemade cookie, Original Toll House® Cookie? Credit for the development of this legendary cookie goes to Ruth Wakefield. According to one of many versions of the tale, it all began in the 1930s when Mrs. Wakefield, proprietress of the Toll House Inn, was preparing a favorite Colonial cookie. She decided to add some chopped chocolate to the batter, thinking it would melt, resulting in chocolate cookies. Much to her surprise, the pieces of chocolate held their shape. The rest is history.

The cookie became so popular for at-home baking that Nestlé started producing a semisweet chocolate bar to use in making them. It was scored into tiny sections for easy division and sold with a special chocolate chopper. In 1939, Nestlé began manufacturing semisweet chocolate morsels as we know them today and the original recipe appeared on the back of the package. The phenomenon which began more than half a century ago is still going strong today.

Brownies, which mean different things to different people, will always hold a special place in the cookie hall of fame. If you find them addictive, we've included several popular variations so you can decide which you like best.

Remember Snickerdoodles, Lemon Squares, Caramelitas or Mincemeat Squares? You'll find them all here, in addition to a chocolate version of layered bars, dubbed Hello Dollies, and the perennial favorite, Rum Balls. Crackle-Top Molasses Cookies with their old-fashioned flavor rank high in popularity with children today.

For a nostalgic glimpse of some of your cookie favorites, flip through the pages. Many recipes will bring back memorable eating experiences.

Original Toll House® Cookies   *Photo on page 81.*

America's favorite cookie originated at New England's Toll House Inn.

1 cup butter, room temperature
3/4 cup granulated sugar
3/4 cup packed brown sugar
1 teaspoon vanilla extract
2 eggs

2-1/4 cups all-purpose flour
1 teaspoon baking soda
1 teaspoon salt
2 cups (12 oz.) semisweet chocolate pieces
1 cup chopped nuts, if desired

Preheat oven to 375F (190C). In a large bowl, beat together butter, granulated sugar, brown sugar, vanilla and eggs until light and fluffy. Add flour, baking soda and salt, beating until well blended. Stir in chocolate pieces and nuts, if desired. Drop by rounded teaspoonfuls, 2 inches apart, on ungreased baking sheets. Bake 8 to 10 minutes or until lightly browned. Remove cookies from baking sheets; cool on racks. Makes 100 (2-inch) cookies.

Variations

Toll House® Pan Cookies: Grease a 15'' x 10'' jelly-roll pan. Prepare dough as directed above. Spread evenly in greased jelly-roll pan. Bake 20 minutes or until golden. Cool in pan. Cut cooled cookies into squares. Makes 35 (2-inch) cookies.
Giant Toll House® Cookies: Prepare dough as directed above. Drop dough by 1/4 cupfuls on ungreased baking sheets. Lightly press into 3-inch circles, placing about 3 inches apart. Bake 10 to 12 minutes or until golden. Remove cookies from baking sheets; cool on racks. Makes about 21 (4-inch) cookies.
Slice & Bake Toll House® Cookies: Prepare dough as directed above. Divide dough into 3 equal portions. Shape each portion into a log 8 inches long. Wrap and refrigerate up to 1 week or freeze up to 2 months. To bake cookies, preheat oven to 375F (190C). Cut each chilled log into 8 (1-inch) slices. Cut each slice into quarters. Place 2 inches apart on ungreased baking sheets. Bake 8 to 10 minutes or until golden. Remove cookies from baking sheets; cool on racks. Makes 96 (2-inch) cookies.
Whole-Wheat Toll House® Cookies: Substitute whole-wheat flour for half the amount of all-purpose flour. Cookies will be darker in color.
Flavor Variations: Omit nuts and add one of the following: 4 cups crisp ready-to-eat cereal, 2 cups chopped pitted dates, 2 cups raisins, 1 cup smooth or crunchy peanut butter, 1 to 1-1/2 cups flaked or shredded coconut or 1 tablespoon grated orange peel.

Rum Balls

A traditional favorite in a variety of flavors.

1 cup (6 oz.) semisweet chocolate pieces, melted
1/3 cup powdered sugar
3 tablespoons corn syrup
1/3 cup rum, bourbon or other liquor or liqueur

2-1/2 cups vanilla-wafer crumbs or chocolate-wafer crumbs
1 cup finely chopped walnuts
2 tablespoons unsweetened cocoa
3 tablespoons granulated sugar

In a medium bowl, combine melted chocolate, powdered sugar, corn syrup and rum, bourbon, liquor or liqueur. Stir in wafer crumbs and walnuts, blending well. Shape into 1-inch balls. In a small bowl, combine cocoa and granulated sugar. Roll balls in cocoa mixture. Store in an airtight container at least 1 day before serving. Makes about 55 (1-inch) balls.

Famous Oatmeal Cookies

An all-time favorite from the Quaker Oats box.

3/4 cup vegetable shortening
1 cup packed brown sugar
1/2 cup granulated sugar
1 egg
1/4 cup water

1 teaspoon vanilla extract
3 cups rolled oats
1 cup all-purpose flour
1/2 teaspoon baking soda
1 teaspoon salt, if desired

Preheat oven to 350F (175C). Grease baking sheets. In a large bowl, beat together shortening, brown sugar, granulated sugar, egg, water and vanilla until creamy. Add rolled oats, flour, baking soda and salt, if desired; combine well. Drop by heaping teaspoonfuls, about 2 inches apart, onto greased baking sheets. Bake 12 to 15 minutes or until golden brown. Remove cookies from baking sheets; cool on racks. Makes about 60 (3-inch) cookies.

Variation

For variety, add 1/2 to 3/4 cup chopped nuts, raisins, semisweet chocolate pieces, or flaked or shredded coconut.

Oatmeal-Cookie Chews

Oatmeal-cookie fans will love this chewy version.

1 cup butter or margarine, room temperature
1 cup packed brown sugar
1 cup granulated sugar
2 teaspoons vanilla extract
1/2 teaspoon salt
3 eggs

2-1/2 cups all-purpose flour
2 teaspoons baking soda
2 cups rolled oats
1 cup raisins
1/2 cup chopped walnuts, if desired
About 1/3 cup granulated sugar

In a large bowl, beat together butter or margarine, brown sugar, 1 cup granulated sugar, vanilla and salt until light and fluffy. Add eggs, one at a time, beating well after each addition. Add flour and baking soda, beating until thoroughly blended. Stir in oats, raisins and walnuts, if desired. Refrigerate dough 1 to 2 hours for easier handling. To bake cookies, preheat oven to 350F (175C). Shape dough into 1-1/2-inch balls. Roll in 1/3 cup granulated sugar, coating completely. Place 3 inches apart on ungreased baking sheets, flattening slightly with bottom of a glass. Bake 10 to 12 minutes or until golden. Cool 1 to 2 minutes on baking sheets; then remove to racks to cool completely. Makes about 50 (3-inch) cookies.

Tip

When a recipe calls for a small amount of toasted nuts, save energy by toasting them in a toaster oven or in a small skillet on top of the stove, rather than heating up your conventional oven.

Calico Cookie Gems

Team peanut butter, oats and colorful candies in these flourless cookies. Children love them.

1/2 cup butter or margarine, room temperature	2 eggs
1-1/4 cups smooth or crunchy peanut butter	2 teaspoons baking soda
1 cup granulated sugar	4 cups rolled oats
1 cup packed brown sugar	2 cups colored-candy-coated chocolate pieces
2 teaspoons vanilla extract	1/2 cup chopped walnuts, if desired

Preheat oven to 350F (175C). In a large bowl, beat together butter or margarine, peanut butter, granulated sugar, brown sugar, vanilla and eggs until light and fluffy. Add baking soda and oats, beating until blended. Stir in 1-1/2 cups candy pieces and walnuts, if desired. Drop by teaspoonfuls, 2 inches apart, on ungreased baking sheets. Flatten cookies slightly with your fingers or bottom of a glass. Press a few of the remaining 1/2 cup candies into top of each cookie. Bake 12 to 14 minutes or until golden brown. Remove cookies from baking sheets; cool on racks. Makes about 50 (2-1/2-inch) cookies.

Caramelitas

Full of caramel topping, chocolate and pecans, these will remind you of chocolate-pecan pie.

1-1/4 cups all-purpose flour	1/2 cup butter or margarine, melted
3/4 cup rolled oats	1 (12.25-oz.) jar caramel topping
1/2 cup packed brown sugar	1 cup (6 oz.) semisweet chocolate pieces
1/2 teaspoon baking soda	1 cup coarsely chopped pecans

Preheat oven to 350F (175C). In a large bowl, beat together 1 cup flour, oats, brown sugar, baking soda and melted butter or margarine until well blended. Press mixture evenly in bottom of an ungreased 13" x 9" baking pan. Bake 10 minutes. Meanwhile, in a small bowl, combine caramel topping and remaining 1/4 cup flour until thoroughly blended. Remove pan from oven. Sprinkle crust with chocolate pieces, then pecans. Drizzle caramel mixture evenly over top. Bake 20 to 25 minutes longer or until bubbly and browned. Cool in pan. Cut cooled cookies into bars. Makes 36 (2-1/8" x 1-1/2") cookies.

S'mores Squares

Reminiscent of those delicious campfire favorites, these are baked in a pan.

1/2 cup butter or margarine, room temperature	3/4 cup all-purpose flour
1/3 cup packed brown sugar	1 cup (6 oz.) semisweet chocolate pieces
3/4 cup graham-cracker crumbs	2 cups miniature marshmallows

Preheat oven to 275F (135C). Grease an 8- or 9-inch-square baking pan. In a medium bowl, beat together butter or margarine and brown sugar until light and fluffy. Add graham-cracker crumbs and flour, beating until well blended. Press mixture evenly in bottom of greased baking pan. Sprinkle evenly with chocolate pieces and marshmallows. Bake 15 to 20 minutes or until light golden. Cool in pan. Cut cooled cookies into squares. Makes 16 (2-inch) cookies.

Snickerdoodles

Cinnamon-sugar coated, these are an old-time family favorite.

Cinnamon-Sugar Coating, see below
1 cup margarine, room temperature
1-1/3 cups sugar
2 eggs

3 cups all-purpose flour
1-1/2 teaspoons cream of tartar
1 teaspoon baking soda
Pinch of salt

Cinnamon-Sugar Coating:
2 tablespoons sugar

1-1/2 teaspoons ground cinnamon

Prepare Cinnamon-Sugar Coating; set aside. Preheat oven to 375F (190C). In a large bowl, beat together margarine, sugar and eggs until fluffy. Add flour, cream of tartar, baking soda and salt, beating until blended. Shape into 1-inch balls. Roll in Cinnamon-Sugar Coating, covering completely. Place 2-1/2 inches apart on ungreased baking sheets. Bake 10 minutes or until golden. Remove cookies from baking sheets; cool on racks. Makes about 80 (2-inch) cookies.

Cinnamon-Sugar Coating:
In a small bowl, combine sugar and cinnamon.

Favorite Peanut-Butter Crackles

These are the best! Good travelers and keepers too!

3/4 cup butter or margarine,
    room temperature
3/4 cup packed brown sugar
3/4 cup granulated sugar
3/4 cup smooth or crunchy peanut butter
1 egg

1 teaspoon vanilla extract
1-3/4 cups all-purpose flour
Pinch of salt
1/2 teaspoon baking soda
About 1/3 cup granulated sugar

Preheat oven to 350F (175C). In a large bowl, beat together butter or margarine, brown sugar and 3/4 cup granulated sugar until creamy. Add peanut butter, egg and vanilla, beating until well blended. Beat in flour, salt and baking soda. Shape rounded teaspoonfuls of dough into 1-1/4-inch balls; then roll in 1/3 cup granulated sugar, covering completely. Place 2 inches apart on ungreased baking sheets. Bake 10 to 12 minutes or until golden. Remove cookies from baking sheets; cool on racks. Makes about 68 (1-3/4-inch) cookies.

Tip

Frozen cookies are best eaten within 1 month, 2 at the most.

Back to front: Original Toll House® Cookies, page 77; Snickerdoodles, above; Crackle-Top Molasses Cookies, page 82; and Peanut-Butter & Jelly Thumbprints, page 85.

Crackle-Top Molasses Cookies *Photo on page 81.*

My son Grant enjoys these crisp cookies that are similar to gingersnaps.

2/3 cup vegetable oil
1 cup sugar
1 egg
1/4 cup molasses
2 to 2-1/4 cups all-purpose flour

2 teaspoons baking soda
1 teaspoon ground cinnamon
1 teaspoon ground ginger
About 1/3 cup sugar

Preheat oven to 350F (175C). In a large bowl, combine oil and 1 cup sugar. Add egg, beating well. Stir in molasses, 2 cups flour, baking soda, cinnamon and ginger. If necessary, add a little more flour to make a firm dough. Shape dough into 1-1/4-inch balls. Roll in 1/3 cup sugar. Place 3 inches apart on ungreased baking sheets. Bake 12 to 14 minutes or until golden brown and tops crack. Remove cookies from baking sheets; cool on racks. Makes about 45 (2-1/2-inch) cookies.

Molasses Softies

Be sure not to overbake these or they will not be soft.

1 cup butter or margarine, room temperature
1-1/3 cups sugar
1 egg
1/3 cup molasses
3 tablespoons dark corn syrup
2 tablespoons milk

4 cups all-purpose flour
2 teaspoons baking soda
2 teaspoons ground cinnamon
1-1/2 teaspoons ground ginger
1-1/2 teaspoons ground cloves
Sugar

Preheat oven to 350F (175C). In a large bowl, beat together butter or margarine, 1-1/3 cups sugar and egg until light and fluffy. Beat in molasses, corn syrup and milk until blended. Add flour, baking soda, cinnamon, ginger and cloves, beating until well blended. Shape dough into 1-1/2-inch balls. Roll balls in sugar. Place 3 inches apart on ungreased baking sheets. Bake 12 to 14 minutes or until golden. **Do not overbake** or cookies will not be soft. Cool 1 to 2 minutes on baking sheets; then remove to racks to cool completely. Makes about 40 (3-inch) cookies.

Chocolate-Chip Butter Cookies

Rich and buttery, these are a delicious chocolate-chip variation.

1 cup butter, room temperature
1 cup powdered sugar
1 teaspoon vanilla extract
1/4 teaspoon salt

2-1/4 cups all-purpose flour
1 cup (6 oz.) semisweet chocolate pieces
Powdered sugar

Preheat oven to 350F (175C). In a medium bowl, beat together butter, 1 cup powdered sugar, vanilla and salt until light and fluffy. Add flour, beating until well blended. Mixture will be stiff. Stir in chocolate pieces. Shape dough into 1-inch balls. Place 2 inches apart on ungreased baking sheets. Flatten with tines of a fork. Bake 15 minutes or until edges begin to brown lightly. Remove cookies from baking sheets; cool on racks. While warm, sift powdered sugar over tops. Makes about 35 (1-3/4-inch) cookies.

Ranger Cookies

This cereal-cookie recipe is easily halved if you want a smaller quantity.

1 cup vegetable shortening
1 cup granulated sugar
3/4 cup packed brown sugar
2 eggs
1-1/2 teaspoons vanilla extract
1/4 teaspoon salt
2 cups all-purpose flour

1-1/2 teaspoons baking soda
3/4 teaspoon baking powder
2 cups rolled oats
2 cups toasted-corn-cereal flakes
3/4 cup flaked or shredded coconut
1/3 cup sunflower nuts, if desired

Preheat oven to 350F (175C). In a large bowl, beat together shortening, granulated sugar, brown sugar, eggs, vanilla and salt until light and fluffy. Add flour, baking soda and baking powder, beating until blended. Stir in oats, cereal flakes, coconut and sunflower nuts, if desired. Drop by rounded teaspoonfuls, 2 inches apart, on ungreased baking sheets. Bake 14 to 16 minutes or until golden. Remove cookies from baking sheets; cool on racks. Makes 85 to 90 (2-inch) cookies.

Lemon Squares

A tangy lemon mixture bakes on top of a buttery cookie crust in these rich lemon-lover treats.

1/2 cup powdered sugar
2 cups all-purpose flour
1 cup butter or margarine
4 eggs
2 cups granulated sugar

1 teaspoon baking powder
1/4 teaspoon salt
2 teaspoons grated lemon peel
1/4 cup fresh lemon juice
Powdered sugar

Preheat oven to 350F (175C). In a small bowl, combine 1/2 cup powdered sugar and flour. Using a fork or pastry blender, cut in butter or margarine until mixture is crumbly and size of small peas. Press mixture evenly in bottom of an ungreased 13" x 9" baking pan. Bake 15 minutes. Meanwhile, in a medium bowl, beat together eggs, granulated sugar, baking powder, salt, lemon peel and lemon juice until fluffy. Pour over hot crust. Bake 20 to 25 minutes longer or until no imprint remains when touched lightly in center. Cool in pan. While hot, sift powdered sugar over top. Refrigerate 4 hours or overnight before cutting. This is an important step. Cut chilled cookies into squares. Store in refrigerator. Makes 48 (1-1/2-inch) cookies.

Tip *Before baking a quantity of cookies, make a test run by baking 2 or 3 cookies. If there is a problem, only a few cookies are ruined. If cookies spread out too far, add a little flour. If dough is too dry or stiff and cookies are too thick, add a little milk or cream. If cookies brown too quickly, reduce oven temperature.*

Exquisite Chocolate-Mint Sticks

Bet you can't eat just one of these. Yummy!

2 oz. unsweetened chocolate
1/2 cup butter or margarine
2 eggs
1 cup granulated sugar
1/4 teaspoon peppermint extract
1/2 cup all-purpose flour

Pinch of salt
1/2 cup chopped unblanched almonds or
  walnuts
Mint Frosting, see below
Chocolate Glaze, see below

Mint Frosting:
3 tablespoons butter or margarine,
  room temperature
1-1/2 cups powdered sugar
1-1/2 to 2 tablespoons cream or milk

1-1/4 teaspoons peppermint extract
2 to 3 drops green food coloring

Chocolate Glaze:
2 oz. unsweetened chocolate

2 tablespoons butter or margarine

Preheat oven to 350F (175C). Grease an 8- or 9-inch-square baking pan. In top of a double boiler, combine chocolate and butter or margarine. Heat over hot but not boiling water until melted and smooth, stirring occasionally. In a medium bowl, beat together eggs, sugar, melted-chocolate mixture and peppermint extract. Add flour and salt, beating until blended. Stir in nuts. Spread in greased pan. Bake 25 to 30 minutes or until set. Do not overbake. Cool in pan. Prepare Mint Frosting. Spread top of cooled brownies with frosting. Refrigerate until frosting is firm. Prepare Chocolate Glaze. Drizzle glaze over frosting; tilt pan until glaze covers surface. Refrigerate 10 minutes; then cut into sticks. Store in refrigerator. Makes about 32 (2" x 1") cookies.

Mint Frosting:
In a medium bowl, beat together butter or margarine, powdered sugar, cream or milk and peppermint extract until smooth and fluffy. Stir in green food coloring.

Chocolate Glaze:
In top of a double boiler, combine chocolate and butter or margarine. Heat over hot but not boiling water until melted and smooth, stirring occasionally.

Chocolate Hello Dollies

Vary the crumbs and nuts in these effortless bars for an entirely different taste.

1/2 cup butter or margarine
1-1/2 cups chocolate-wafer crumbs or
  graham-cracker crumbs
1-1/2 cups flaked or shredded coconut

1-1/2 cups chopped almonds, pecans or
  walnuts
1 cup (6 oz.) semisweet chocolate pieces
1 (14-oz.) can sweetened condensed milk

Preheat oven to 350F (175C). Place butter or margarine in a 13" x 9" baking pan. Heat in oven until melted, watching carefully. Remove pan from oven; stir in crumbs until thoroughly moistened. Spread evenly in pan, pressing gently with back of a fork to form crust. Sprinkle coconut evenly over crumb mixture; then sprinkle with nuts and chocolate pieces. Drizzle sweetened condensed milk evenly over top. Bake 25 to 30 minutes or until lightly browned. Cool in pan. Cut cooled cookies into bars. Makes 40 (1-3/4" x 1-1/2") cookies.

How to Make Peanut-Butter & Chocolate Kisses

1/Shape rounded teaspoonfuls of dough into balls; roll in granulated sugar. Place 2 inches apart on ungreased baking sheets.

2/After removing cookies from oven, immediately top each cookie with a chocolate candy kiss, carefully pressing down firmly.

Peanut-Butter & Chocolate Kisses

Peanut-butter and chocolate lovers will have a hard time resisting these.

1/2 cup butter or margarine, room temperature	**1 teaspoon vanilla extract**
1/2 cup smooth or crunchy peanut butter	**1/4 teaspoon salt**
3/4 cup packed brown sugar	**1-3/4 cups all-purpose flour**
1/4 cup granulated sugar	**1 teaspoon baking soda**
1 egg	**3 tablespoons granulated sugar**
	48 milk-chocolate candy kisses, unwrapped

Preheat oven to 375F (190C). In a medium bowl, beat together butter or margarine, peanut butter, brown sugar, 1/4 cup granulated sugar, egg, vanilla and salt until light and fluffy. Add flour and baking soda, beating until thoroughly blended. Shape dough into 48 balls, using a rounded teaspoon for each. Roll balls in 3 tablespoons granulated sugar. Place 2 inches apart on ungreased baking sheets. Bake 8 to 10 minutes or until light golden. Immediately top each cookie with a candy kiss, carefully pressing down firmly. Remove cookies from baking sheets; cool on racks. Makes 48 (1-3/4-inch) cookies.

Variation

Peanut-Butter & Jelly Thumbprints: *Photo on page 81.* Prepare dough as directed above. Shape dough into 48 balls. Do not roll balls in sugar. Place balls 2 inches apart on ungreased baking sheets. Bake as directed. Immediately upon removal from oven, make an imprint with a wooden-spoon handle in center of each cookie. Fill center of each thumbprint with 1/4 teaspoon strawberry preserves or raspberry jam. Remove cookies from baking sheets; cool on racks. Makes 48 (1-3/4-inch) cookies.

Sinfully Rich Fudgy Brownies

A chocolate-marshmallow topping makes these fudgy brownies sinfully delicious.

4 oz. unsweetened chocolate	1 tablespoon vanilla extract
1 cup butter	1/4 teaspoon salt
4 eggs	1 cup all-purpose flour
2 cups granulated sugar	Chocolate-Marshmallow Frosting, see below

Chocolate-Marshmallow Frosting:

4 oz. unsweetened chocolate	1 tablespoon vanilla extract
1 cup butter	1 (1-lb.) pkg. powdered sugar (3-3/4 cups)
2 eggs	4 cups miniature marshmallows

Preheat oven to 350F (175C). Grease a 13" x 9" baking pan. In a large saucepan, combine chocolate and butter. Heat over low heat until melted and smooth, stirring occasionally. Remove from heat. Beat in eggs, granulated sugar, vanilla and salt until thoroughly blended. Stir in flour, blending well. Spread evenly in bottom of greased baking pan. Bake 25 to 30 minutes. Brownies should be moist. Do not overbake. Cool in pan. Meanwhile, prepare Chocolate-Marshmallow Frosting. While frosting is slightly warm, spread brownies with Chocolate-Marshmallow Frosting. Refrigerate several hours or overnight. Cut chilled cookies into bars. Store in refrigerator. Makes 40 (1-3/4" x 1-1/2") brownies.

Chocolate-Marshmallow Frosting:
In a medium saucepan, combine chocolate and butter. Heat over low heat until melted and smooth, stirring occasionally. Remove from heat. Add eggs, vanilla and powdered sugar, beating until smooth. Stir in marshmallows.

Quick Brownies

Brownies I grew up on. They can be made in minutes for a quick chocolate treat.

1/2 cup butter or margarine, room temperature	1 teaspoon vanilla extract
1 cup sugar	2 oz. unsweetened chocolate, melted
2 eggs	2/3 cup all-purpose flour
	3/4 to 1 cup chopped walnuts

Preheat oven to 325F (165C). Grease an 8- or 9-inch-square baking pan. In a medium bowl, beat together butter or margarine, sugar, eggs and vanilla until light and fluffy. Beat in melted chocolate. Add flour, beating until well blended. Stir in walnuts. Spread evenly in greased baking pan. Bake 25 to 30 minutes. Do not overbake. Cool in pan. Cut cooled brownies into squares. Makes 16 (2-inch) brownies.

Variations

Orange Brownies: Stir in 1 tablespoon grated orange peel along with walnuts. Proceed as directed above.

Chocolate-Frosted Brownies: Bake brownies as directed. Cool 10 minutes. Spread brownies evenly with Chocolate Frosting. To prepare Chocolate Frosting, place 1 cup (6 ounces) semisweet chocolate pieces in blender. In small saucepan, heat 1/2 cup whipping cream until hot. Quickly pour cream into blender. Add 1 teaspoon vanilla extract; blend until chocolate melts and mixture is smooth and glossy. Refrigerate until set before cutting into squares. Store in refrigerator.

Brownies Supreme

Corn syrup helps make these wonderful brownies chewy.

1 cup butter or margarine, room temperature
8 oz. unsweetened chocolate
6 eggs
3 cups granulated sugar
1/2 cup dark corn syrup

1-1/2 cups all-purpose flour
1 tablespoon vanilla extract
1-1/2 to 2 cups chopped walnuts
2 recipes Fudge Frosting, page 101,
    if desired, or powdered sugar

Preheat oven to 350F (175C). Grease and flour or line a 15" x 10" jelly-roll pan with foil. In a medium saucepan, combine butter or margarine and chocolate. Heat over low heat until melted and smooth, stirring occasionally; cool. In a large bowl, beat together eggs and granulated sugar. Beat in cooled chocolate mixture. Add corn syrup, flour and vanilla, beating until well blended. Stir in walnuts. Spread evenly in greased or foil-lined jelly-roll pan. Bake 25 to 30 minutes. Do not overbake. Brownies should be moist in center. Cool in pan. Prepare Fudge Frosting, if desired. Spread Fudge Frosting evenly over top of cooled brownies. Or, sift powdered sugar over top. Cut cooled brownies into squares. Makes about 48 (1-3/4-inch) brownies.

Variation

Substitute 1-1/2 cups unsweetened cocoa for unsweetened chocolate. Increase butter to 1-1/4 cups. Proceed as directed above.

Mincemeat Squares

A no-fuss square to assist in making holiday baking a breeze.

1/4 cup butter or margarine
3/4 cup packed brown sugar
1 egg
1/2 teaspoon brandy extract or
    vanilla extract

Pinch of salt
2/3 cup prepared mincemeat
1 cup all-purpose flour
1 teaspoon baking powder
Brandy Glaze, see below

Brandy Glaze:
1/2 cup powdered sugar
1 tablespoon butter or margarine,
    room temperature

1 tablespoon brandy or orange juice

Preheat oven to 350F (175C). Grease an 8- or 9-inch-square baking pan. In a medium saucepan, melt butter or margarine over low heat. Remove from heat. Stir in brown sugar, egg, brandy extract or vanilla and salt, blending well. Stir in mincemeat. Add flour and baking powder, blending well. Spread evenly in greased baking pan. Bake 30 to 35 minutes or until a wooden pick inserted in center comes out clean. Cool in pan. Meanwhile, prepare Brandy Glaze. While cookies are slightly warm, spread with Brandy Glaze. When glaze has set, cut into squares. Makes 25 (1-1/2-inch) cookies.

Brandy Glaze:
In a small bowl, combine powdered sugar, butter or margarine and brandy or juice until smooth.

How to Make Grandpa's Fruit Bars

1/Using floured hands, shape dough into a log 11 inches long, 1-1/2 inches wide and 1/2 inch thick.

2/Cool baked logs 10 minutes on sheets. Then with a sharp knife, cut diagonally into 1-inch bars.

Grandpa's Fruit Bars

My version of my husband's favorite recipe from his grandfather, a professional baker.

3/4 cup raisins
1/2 cup chopped pitted dates
2 tablespoons brandy or orange juice
1/2 cup butter or margarine, room
    temperature, or vegetable shortening
1/2 cup granulated sugar
1/2 cup packed brown sugar
2 eggs, 1 separated

1 teaspoon vanilla extract
1 teaspoon ground cinnamon
1/4 teaspoon ground nutmeg
1-3/4 cups all-purpose flour
1/2 teaspoon baking soda
1 cup coarsely chopped walnuts
1/2 teaspoon water

In a small bowl, combine raisins, dates and brandy or orange juice; set aside. Preheat oven to 375F (190C). Grease 2 baking sheets. In a large bowl, beat together butter or margarine or shortening, granulated sugar, brown sugar, 1 egg, 1 egg white and vanilla until light and fluffy. Beat in cinnamon, nutmeg, flour and baking soda until thoroughly blended. Stir in raisin mixture and walnuts. Divide dough into 4 equal portions. Place 2 portions on each baking sheet. Using floured hands, shape each portion into a log 11 inches long, 1-1/2 inches wide and 1/2 inch thick. Stir together remaining egg yolk and water. Using pastry brush, brush top of logs with egg wash. Bake 12 to 15 minutes or until light golden. Logs will feel soft but will become firm upon cooling. Cool 10 minutes on baking sheets; then with a sharp knife, cut diagonally into 1-inch bars. Cool completely on baking sheets. Makes about 44 (1-inch) cookies.

Entertaining & Holiday Cookies

Busy hostesses love to present festive trays of colorful cookies—dazzling delights that are a feast for the eyes as well as the palate. This chapter is designed to help you with just that—and to take the hassle out of entertaining. It's filled with fabulous, show-off creations that guests can't resist. Geared for entertaining the year round, these contemporary cookies will fit into any memorable holiday-feasting plans.

Pick your time schedule and entertaining considerations. If you are making sweets for a large gathering, be sure to include variety. If necessary, bake three or four different kinds of cookies in advance and store in the freezer. Or, make the dough well ahead of party time and freeze. Then bake cookies in your spare moments a few days prior to the party.

Coordinate your cookie trays, varying them in size and shape. Select cookies with regard to style, shape, color, flavor and texture. Mix and match them for the most attractive, colorful and interesting platters. On some trays you might want to arrange different cookie styles. On others, particularly small trays, you might want to make a single cookie type the star. Always present cookies attractively. Arrange them neatly in rows, concentric circles or pretty designs. Make plates a mosaic of pretty colors and delicious flavors.

This enticing kaleidoscope of sweet gems includes Sugarplum Squares, rich two-layer delicacies made with a buttery crust and coconut-raisin topping. Holiday Almond Bon Bons and Chocolate-Cherry Bon Bons are made to order for almond-paste, chocolate and cherry lovers.

The recipe for almond Florentines, shared by a professional baker, yields the ultimate in fabulous cookie creations and is one of my very favorites. Baking them in large or small foil pans is the trick to getting them out all in one piece. Coated with chocolate, the giant rounds make sensational holiday gifts.

When thoughts turn to gift-giving and creating special foods, consider the array of ideas here. The best-remembered presents are often those created with your own hands.

Butter-Mint Patties

Use your food processor to whip up these four-ingredient mint patties in minutes.

1 cup butter mints
1 cup butter, room temperature

2 cups all-purpose flour
1 tablespoon sugar

In a food processor fitted with a steel blade, process butter mints until crushed. Add butter and flour. Process until dough forms. If necessary, refrigerate dough 1 hour for ease in handling. Preheat oven to 300F (150C). On a floured piece of waxed paper, roll dough into a 9-inch square. Sprinkle with sugar. Cut into 36 (1-1/2-inch) squares. Using tiny hors d'oeuvre or cookie cutters, press a design on each square, being careful not to cut through bottom of cookie. Place 1-1/2 inches apart on ungreased baking sheets. Bake 18 to 20 minutes or until bottoms are pale golden. Do not overbake. Remove cookies from baking sheets; cool on racks. Makes 36 (2-inch) cookies.

Florentine Triangle Jewels   *Photo on page 103.*

A florentine mixture bakes on top of a butter crust to complete these colorful treats.

Buttery Crust, see below
3/4 cup butter
1/2 cup granulated sugar
1/4 cup whipping cream
1/2 cup chopped red candied cherries
1/2 cup chopped green candied cherries

1/2 cup chopped candied pineapple
1 cup sliced blanched almonds
2 tablespoons grated orange peel
1/2 cup (3 oz.) semisweet chocolate pieces,
  melted

Buttery Crust:
1-1/2 cups all-purpose flour
1/2 cup powdered sugar
1/2 cup butter, cut into pieces

2 teaspoons vanilla extract
2 tablespoons whipping cream

Line a 15" x 10" jelly-roll pan with foil. Prepare Buttery Crust. Press crust mixture evenly into bottom of foil-lined pan. Refrigerate while preparing topping. Preheat oven to 375F (190C). In a medium saucepan, combine butter, granulated sugar and cream. Place over medium heat; cook until mixture boils, stirring often. Boil 1 to 2 minutes, stirring constantly. Stir in candied cherries, candied pineapple, almonds and orange peel. Spread mixture evenly over chilled crust. Bake 15 to 20 minutes or until golden. Cool in pan. While slightly warm, drizzle with chocolate. Allow chocolate to set. Cut cooled cookies into 5 lengthwise strips. Cut each strip into about 13 triangles. Store in refrigerator, if desired. Makes 65 to 70 (2-inch) cookies.

Buttery Crust:
In a food processor fitted with a steel blade, combine flour, powdered sugar and butter. Process until blended. With motor running, add vanilla and cream through feed tube, processing until dough begins to cling together.

Tip
A fork is helpful in drizzling chocolate. Simply dip fork in melted chocolate. Allow chocolate to run off fork in random pattern over cookies.

Almond Florentines

Sensational describes these candy-like cookie confections.

1 cup butter
1 cup sugar
1/3 cup honey
1/3 cup whipping cream

4 cups sliced blanched almonds
1 cup (6 oz.) semisweet chocolate pieces,
melted

Preheat oven to 375F (190C). Grease 6 (8-inch) foil pie pans. Foil pans must be used for easy removal of baked florentines in 1 piece. In a medium, heavy saucepan, combine butter, sugar, honey and whipping cream. Heat to boiling over medium heat, stirring frequently. Cook 1-1/2 minutes, stirring constantly. Remove from heat. Stir in almonds. Divide mixture evenly among greased pie pans. Using fingers, dipped often in cold water, pat mixture evenly onto bottom of pans. Bake 10 to 14 minutes or until a rich golden brown. Cool completely in pans. Refrigerate 5 to 10 minutes for ease in removing from pans. With fingers, carefully press in pan bottoms from underneath and pop florentines out in 1 piece. Refrigerate stacked between layers of waxed paper. Spread bottom sides of chilled florentines with melted chocolate. Let stand until chocolate sets. Store in refrigerator. Makes 6 (6-1/2-inch) cookies.

Variation

To make smaller florentines, grease 16 (4-1/2-inch) foil tart pans. Proceed as directed above, dividing mixture evenly among greased tart pans. Makes 16 (3-inch) cookies.

Tip

Chocolate-coating wafers, available at cake- or candy-decorating-supply stores, are ideal for melting and spreading on bottom sides of florentines.

Almond-Paste Crescents

Use a large pastry bag fitted with an open-star decorating tube to shape these elegant macaroons.

2/3 cup powdered sugar
1/3 cup granulated sugar
1 tablespoon all-purpose flour
1 (7-oz.) pkg. almond paste,
cut into pieces

2 egg whites
1/4 teaspoon almond extract
1/2 cup sliced or slivered blanched almonds

Preheat oven to 350F (175C). Grease a baking sheet. In a medium bowl, combine powdered sugar, granulated sugar and flour. Add almond paste, egg whites and almond extract. Beat with electric mixer at medium speed until thoroughly blended and smooth. Place dough in a large pastry bag fitted with a large open-star 3/4-inch-diameter decorating tube, filling bag half-full at a time. Pipe dough into 2-3/4-inch crescents, 1 inch apart, on greased baking sheet. Sprinkle with almonds. Bake 15 minutes or until edges are light golden. Remove cookies from baking sheet; cool on racks. Makes about 20 (2-1/4-inch) cookies.

How to Make Almond Florentines

1/Divide almond mixture among greased pie pans.

2/Using your fingers, pat mixture evenly in pans.

3/With your fingers, press in each pan bottom to remove florentines.

4/Spread bottom of each chilled florentine with melted chocolate.

Layered Almond-Paste Cookies

Make your own almond paste to use in these layered cookies.

Almond Paste, see below
3/4 cup butter or margarine,
   room temperature
1/3 cup powdered sugar
1 teaspoon vanilla extract

1 egg
2 cups all-purpose flour
1 teaspoon baking powder
Chocolate Glaze, see below

Almond Paste:
1-1/2 cups whole or slivered
   blanched almonds
1-1/3 cups powdered sugar

1 egg white
1 to 1-1/4 teaspoons almond extract
1/4 teaspoon salt

Chocolate Glaze:
1 cup (6 oz.) semisweet chocolate pieces
1 tablespoon butter or margarine

2 teaspoons light corn syrup

Prepare Almond Paste. Between 2 sheets of waxed paper, roll Almond Paste into a 12" x 8" rectangle; set aside. Preheat oven to 350F (175C). Grease a 13" x 9" baking pan. In a large bowl, beat together butter or margarine, powdered sugar, vanilla, egg, flour and baking powder until mixture begins to form a dough. Set aside 1 cup dough. Press remaining dough evenly in bottom of greased baking pan. Lay Almond-Paste rectangle over dough. Divide reserved 1 cup dough into 12 pieces. Roll into 5 ropes, each measuring 12 inches long and 7 ropes, each measuring 8 inches long. Arrange ropes, about 1 inch apart, in a lattice pattern over filling, placing 12-inch ropes down long side of pan and 8-inch ropes across short side of pan. Bake 20 to 25 minutes. Cool in pan. Prepare Chocolate Glaze. Immediately spoon Chocolate Glaze in spaces between lattice ropes. When glaze has set, cut into squares. Makes about 40 (1-1/2-inch) cookies.

Almond Paste:
In a food processor fitted with a steel blade, grind about 3/4 cup almonds; then add remaining almonds until chopped fine. Add powdered sugar; process until combined. Add egg white, almond extract and salt, processing until mixture forms a ball. Makes about 1-1/3 cups.

Chocolate Glaze:
In top of a double boiler, combine chocolate pieces and butter or margarine. Heat over hot but not boiling water until melted and smooth, stirring occasionally. Stir in corn syrup.

Variation
Omit Chocolate Glaze, filling spaces between lattice ropes with raspberry or apricot jam, using about 1/2 cup.

Tip

A food processor is a time- and labor-saver for chopping fruit and nuts. When doing a lot of baking, chop a large batch of nuts at the same time. Store in the freezer until needed.

Buttery Nut Rosettes   *Photo on pages 154 and 155*

A versatile cookie — vary the color and flavor of the dough as well as the frosting garnish.

1 cup butter, room temperature	**1-3/4 cups all-purpose flour**
3/4 cup sugar	**1 cup finely chopped or ground walnuts**
1 egg yolk	**Chocolate-Buttercream Icing, or**
1-1/2 teaspoons vanilla extract	**Vanilla-Buttercream Icing, page 153**
1 to 2 teaspoons grated orange peel, if desired	

Preheat oven to 350F (175C). In a medium bowl, beat together butter, sugar, egg yolk, vanilla and orange peel, if desired, until light and fluffy. Gradually add flour and walnuts, beating until blended. Drop dough by teaspoonfuls, 2 inches apart, on ungreased baking sheets. Or, place dough in a large pastry bag fitted with a large open-star 3/4-inch-diameter decorating tube, filling bag half-full at a time. Pipe dough into 1-1/2-inch-diameter cookies, 2 inches apart, on ungreased baking sheets. Bake 15 minutes or until very lightly browned. Cool 5 minutes on pans; then remove to racks to cool completely. Prepare Chocolate-Buttercream Icing or Vanilla-Buttercream Icing. Frost center of each cooled cookie with a star of icing, using a pastry bag fitted with a small star decorating tube. Let stand until set. Makes about 40 (2- to 2-1/4-inch) cookies.

Variation

Chocolate-Nut Rosettes: Add 1/4 cup unsweetened cocoa to butter-egg mixture before adding flour. Proceed as directed above.

Vienna Squares   *Photo on page 103.*

An elegant old-world-style cookie with a raspberry- or apricot-jam filling.

1 cup unsalted butter, room temperature	**4 egg whites**
1-1/2 cups granulated sugar	**1 tablespoon orange-flavor liqueur or**
2 egg yolks	**bourbon or 1 teaspoon vanilla extract**
1 teaspoon vanilla extract	**2 cups chopped walnuts**
2-1/2 cups all-purpose flour	**1-1/4 cups raspberry or apricot jam**
1/4 teaspoon salt	**Powdered sugar**

Preheat oven to 350F (175C). Grease a 15" x 10" jelly-roll pan. In a large bowl, beat together butter, 1/2 cup granulated sugar, egg yolks and vanilla until light and fluffy. Add flour and salt, beating until blended. Spread dough evenly in bottom of greased jelly-roll pan. Bake 10 minutes. Meanwhile, in a medium bowl, beat egg whites with electric mixer on high speed until stiff, gradually beating in remaining 1 cup granulated sugar and liqueur, bourbon or vanilla. Fold in walnuts. Spread jam evenly over hot baked crust. Carefully top with egg-white mixture, spreading evenly. Bake 30 minutes or until set. While warm, sift powdered sugar over top and cut into squares. Garnish as desired. Cool in pan. Makes 54 (1-5/8-inch) cookies.

Raisin-Tart Squares

These rich buttery squares are reminiscent of chess pie.

Brown-Sugar Crust, see below
1/2 cup granulated sugar
1/2 cup packed brown sugar
2 eggs
1 teaspoon vanilla extract

2 tablespoons all-purpose flour
1/2 teaspoon baking powder
1 cup raisins, plumped in hot water, drained
1/2 cup chopped walnuts
Powdered sugar

Brown-Sugar Crust:
1 cup all-purpose flour
3 tablespoons packed brown sugar
1/2 cup butter or margarine,
   cut into pieces, room temperature

2 teaspoons vanilla extract

Preheat oven to 350F (175C). Prepare Brown-Sugar Crust. Press dough evenly in bottom of an ungreased 8- or 9-inch-square baking pan. Bake 15 minutes or until lightly browned. In a medium bowl, combine granulated sugar, brown sugar, eggs, vanilla, flour and baking powder until well blended. Stir in raisins and walnuts. Spread mixture evenly over hot baked crust. Bake 25 to 30 minutes or until golden brown. Cool in pan. Sift powdered sugar over top. Cut cooled cookies into squares. Makes about 25 (1-1/2-inch) cookies.

Brown-Sugar Crust:
Place flour, brown sugar and butter or margarine in a food processor fitted with a steel blade. Process until blended. With motor running, add vanilla through feed tube. Process until dough begins to cling together in a ball.

Sugarplum Squares

When visions of sugarplums dance in your head, try these holiday favorites.

1 cup all-purpose flour
1-1/4 cups granulated sugar
1/3 cup butter or margarine,
   room temperature
2 eggs
2 tablespoons all-purpose flour
1/2 teaspoon baking powder

1/4 teaspoon salt
1 tablespoon grated orange peel
2 tablespoons orange juice
1/2 cup raisins
3/4 cup chopped walnuts
1 cup flaked or shredded coconut
Powdered sugar

Preheat oven to 350F (175C). Grease an 8- or 9-inch-square baking pan. In a medium bowl, beat together 1 cup flour, 1/4 cup granulated sugar and butter or margarine until well blended. Press mixture evenly in bottom of greased baking pan. Bake 15 minutes or until very lightly browned. Meanwhile, in a medium bowl, beat together eggs, remaining 1 cup granulated sugar, 2 tablespoons flour, baking powder and salt until smooth. Stir in orange peel, orange juice, raisins, walnuts and coconut. Pour mixture over hot baked layer, spreading evenly. Bake 20 to 25 minutes or until lightly browned. Cool in pan. Cut cooled cookies into squares. Sift powdered sugar over top. Makes about 25 (1-1/2-inch) cookies.

How to Make Marzipan Peaches

1/Prepare Peach Sugar in a blender or food processor. Roll dough balls in Peach Sugar. Place on ungreased baking sheets.

2/Garnish each baked cookie with a green-gumdrop piece and a clove "stem."

Marzipan Peaches   Photo on page 103.

Almond-flavored dough coated with gold sugar to look like peaches.

1/4 recipe Basic Almond-Paste Cookie Dough, page 117
Peach Sugar, see below

15 green gumdrops, each cut in quarters
60 whole cloves

Peach Sugar:
1/2 cup sugar
3 drops red food coloring

6 drops yellow food coloring

Refrigerate Basic Almond-Paste Cookie-Dough at least 1 hour. To bake cookies, preheat oven to 350F (175C). Prepare Peach Sugar; set aside. Shape dough into 3/4-inch balls. Roll balls in Peach Sugar, coating completely. Place 1-1/2 inches apart on ungreased baking sheets. Bake 12 to 14 minutes or until bottoms are golden. Remove cookies from baking sheets; cool on racks. Attach a gumdrop piece to each cooled peach cookie with a clove "stem." Makes 60 (1-inch) cookies.

Peach Sugar:
In a food processor fitted with a steel blade, process sugar and colorings until evenly colored.

Chocolate-Cherry Bon Bons   *Photo on page 103.*

A surprise cherry center can be found in these bon bons.

1/4 recipe Basic Almond-Paste Cookie
   Dough, page 117
	1-1/2 cups (9 oz.) semisweet
	   chocolate pieces

24 whole maraschino cherries, well-drained, cut into halves	2 tablespoons butter
1/2 cup whipping cream	1 teaspoon vanilla extract
	1/4 cup chopped pistachio nuts

Preheat oven to 375F (190C). Line 48 (1-3/4-inch) miniature muffin cups with 1-1/2-inch bon-bon papers or small baking cups. Cut Basic Almond-Paste Cookie Dough into 48 equal portions. Flatten each portion of dough in palm of 1 hand with your finger tips; then wrap around a cherry half, enclosing completely. Place in baking cups, flattening tops slightly with your finger tips. Bake 10 to 12 minutes or until beginning to brown lightly. Cool in pans. In a small saucepan, combine cream and chocolate pieces. Heat over low heat until melted and smooth, stirring frequently. Stir in butter and vanilla. Cool until spreading consistency. Spread chocolate over cooled cookies. Sprinkle with pistachio nuts. Store in refrigerator. Makes 48 (1-1/2-inch) cookies.

Holiday Almond Bon Bons

Almond paste on top of a cookie crust makes these bon bons a fabulous holiday treat.

1/2 cup butter, room temperature	1-1/4 cups all-purpose flour
1/2 cup sugar	Almond Filling, see below
1/2 teaspoon vanilla extract	48 red candied cherries
1/4 teaspoon salt	Chocolate Glaze, see below

Almond Filling:

1 (7-oz.) pkg. or 1 (8-oz.) can almond paste	1/4 cup butter, room temperature
1/4 cup sugar	2 eggs

Chocolate Glaze:

1 oz. unsweetened chocolate	1 tablespoon milk
1 tablespoon butter	1/2 teaspoon vanilla extract
1/2 cup powdered sugar	

Preheat oven to 350F (175C). Grease a 13" x 9" baking pan. In a medium bowl, beat together butter, sugar, vanilla and salt until light and fluffy. Gradually beat in flour, only until blended. Press mixture evenly in bottom of greased baking pan. Bake 12 to 14 minutes or until edges begin to brown lightly. Meanwhile, prepare Almond Filling. Spread filling evenly over hot crust. Arrange cherries on filling in 6 rows of 8, spacing evenly. Do not press cherries down. Bake 20 to 25 minutes. Cool in pan. Prepare Chocolate Glaze. Drizzle glaze over cooled cookies. When glaze has set, cut into 48 pieces with a cherry in center of each. Makes 48 (1-1/2-inch) cookies.

Almond Filling:

In a medium bowl, beat together almond paste, sugar and butter with electric mixer until well blended. Beat in eggs until mixture is smooth.

Chocolate Glaze:

In a small saucepan over low heat, melt together chocolate and butter. Remove from heat; stir in powdered sugar, milk and vanilla until smooth.

How to Make Chocolate-Cherry Bon Bons

1/Flatten each dough portion in palm of your hand; then wrap around a cherry half, enclosing completely.

2/Spread tops of cooled cookies generously with chocolate topping.

3/Sprinkle bon bons with chopped pistachio nuts.

4/Refrigerate bon bons until ready to serve.

Zucchini-Fruitcake Bars

When you have a garden full of zucchini, try these moist cake-like bars.

1 cup dark or golden raisins	1 teaspoon ground allspice
1/2 cup chopped pitted dates	1/2 teaspoon ground nutmeg
1/2 cup chopped dried apricots	1/2 teaspoon ground cloves
1/4 cup brandy or rum	1 teaspoon baking soda
2 eggs	1/4 teaspoon baking powder
1/3 cup vegetable oil	1/4 teaspoon salt
1 cup packed brown sugar	1 cup grated unpeeled zucchini
1-1/2 teaspoons vanilla extract	1 cup coarsely chopped walnuts
1-1/2 cups all-purpose flour	Brandy Icing, see below
1-1/2 teaspoons ground cinnamon	40 candied-cherry halves

Brandy Icing:

1/4 cup butter or margarine, room temperature	1 to 2 tablespoons orange juice
3/4 cup powdered sugar	1/4 teaspoon brandy extract

In a small saucepan over medium heat, heat together raisins, dates, apricots and brandy or rum 5 minutes or until most of liquid is absorbed; set aside. Preheat oven to 325F (165C). Grease and flour a 13" x 9" baking pan. In a large bowl, beat together eggs, oil, brown sugar and vanilla until well blended. Beat in flour, cinnamon, allspice, nutmeg, cloves, baking soda, baking powder and salt. Stir in zucchini, nuts and fruit mixture. Spread evenly in greased baking pan. Bake 38 to 42 minutes or until a wooden pick inserted in center comes out clean. Do not overbake. Cool in pan. Prepare Brandy Icing. Frost top evenly with Brandy Icing. When icing has set, cut into bars. Top each with a candied-cherry half. Makes 40 (1-3/4" x 1-1/2") cookies.

Brandy Icing:

In a small bowl, beat together butter or margarine, powdered sugar, orange juice and brandy extract until smooth.

Pumpkin Tea Cakes

Moist, fragrant bites are a nice coffee or tea accompaniment.

1/4 cup vegetable oil	Pinch of salt
1 egg	1/4 teaspoon ground cinnamon
3/4 cup sugar	1/4 teaspoon ground cloves
1/2 cup canned or cooked fresh pumpkin	1/4 teaspoon ground nutmeg
1/4 cup water	1/2 cup chopped pecans
3/4 cup all-purpose flour	1/2 cup chopped pitted dates
1/2 teaspoon baking soda	42 pecan halves
1/8 teaspoon baking powder	

Preheat oven to 350F (175C). Line 42 (1-3/4-inch) miniature muffin cups with 1-1/2-inch bon bon papers or small baking cups. In a medium bowl, combine oil, egg, sugar, pumpkin and water. Add flour, baking soda, baking powder, salt, cinnamon, cloves and nutmeg, blending well. Stir in chopped pecans and dates. Spoon into paper baking cups, filling almost full. Top each with a pecan half. Bake 15 to 17 minutes or until a wooden pick inserted in center comes out clean. Remove from muffin cups; cool on racks. Makes about 42 (1-1/2-inch) tea cakes.

Walnut-Fudge Delights

A baked nut base sports a yummy fudge topping. Elegant and easy!

2 cups ground walnuts or hazelnuts
1/2 cup sugar
2 egg whites

Fudge Frosting, see below
25 walnut halves or hazelnuts

Fudge Frosting:
1/2 cup sugar
1 tablespoon cornstarch
2 oz. unsweetened chocolate, broken up
Pinch of salt

1/2 cup milk
1-1/2 tablespoons butter
1/2 teaspoon vanilla extract

Preheat oven to 350F (175C). Grease an 8- or 9-inch-square baking pan. In a small bowl, combine ground nuts and sugar. Stir in unbeaten egg whites until blended. Press mixture evenly in bottom of greased baking pan. Bake 15 to 17 minutes or until edges are lightly browned. Cool in pan. Prepare Fudge Frosting. Spread top with Fudge Frosting and arrange walnut halves or hazelnuts evenly in 5 rows of 5. Refrigerate. Cut chilled cookies into 25 squares with a nut in center of each. Store in refrigerator. Makes 25 (1-1/2-inch) cookies.

Fudge Frosting:
In a small saucepan, combine sugar and cornstarch; add chocolate and salt. Stir in milk. Cook over medium heat until mixture is smooth, boils and thickens, stirring constantly. Remove from heat. Stir in butter and vanilla until butter melts.

Fudgy Cream-Cheese Sandwich Bars

These delicious bars freeze well.

1 (8-oz.) pkg. cream cheese
2 cups (12 oz.) semisweet chocolate pieces
1 (5.33-oz.) can evaporated milk (2/3 cup)
1 cup chopped walnuts

2 cups all-purpose flour
2/3 cup sugar
2/3 cup butter or margarine, melted
1/2 teaspoon vanilla extract

Preheat oven to 375F (190C). In a medium saucepan, combine cream cheese, chocolate pieces and evaporated milk. Cook over low heat until smooth, stirring constantly. Stir in walnuts; set aside. In a food processor fitted with a steel blade, combine flour and sugar; process until blended. With motor running, pour melted butter or margarine and vanilla through feed tube. With on/off motion, process until crumbly. Remove 1-1/4 cups mixture for topping. Press remainder evenly in bottom of an ungreased 13" x 9" baking pan. Spread chocolate mixture evenly over crust. Sprinkle with reserved crumbly mixture, pressing in gently. Bake 30 minutes or until lightly browned. Cool in pan. Cut cooled cookies into bars. Store in refrigerator. Makes about 40 (1-3/4" x 1-1/2") cookies.

Tip
Come holiday-time, freeze a variety of cookies on a foil-covered piece of cardboard. Overwrap with foil, then wrap with moisture- and vapor-proof paper and seal securely. You can save yourself the trouble of opening and closing several storage containers of frozen cookies and have an attractive tray of cookies to present on a moment's notice.

Chocolate-Pecan Tassies

Try these miniature tarts when time is not at a premium.

1/2 recipe Cream-Cheese Pastry, page 116	Pinch of salt
1 egg	1 oz. unsweetened chocolate, melted
3/4 cup packed brown sugar	3/4 cup chopped pecans
1 tablespoon butter, melted	24 pecan halves
1 teaspoon vanilla extract	

Wrap and refrigerate Cream-Cheese Pastry several hours. Preheat oven to 350F (175C). In a medium bowl, combine egg, brown sugar, butter, vanilla and salt until blended. Stir in chocolate until blended. Stir in chopped pecans; set aside. Divide Cream-Cheese Pastry into 24 equal portions. Press each dough portion evenly in bottom and up sides of an ungreased 2- to 3-inch miniature fluted tart pan. Spoon scant tablespoon pecan mixture into each pastry-lined tart pan. Top with pecan half. Place tart pans, 1 inch apart, on baking sheets. Bake 20 to 25 minutes or until set. Cool slightly in pans; then with a sharp knife loosen edges to release tarts from pans. Cool on racks. Makes 24 (2-to 3-inch) cookie tarts.

Variation

Cranberry-Pecan Miniatures: Omit melted butter and chocolate. Decrease chopped pecans to 3 tablespoons. Stir in 1/3 cup finely chopped cranberries along with chopped pecans.

Apricot-Strudel Slices

For variety, try different fillings.

1/2 cup butter, room temperature	1 cup chopped pecans
1 cup dairy sour cream	2 tablespoons butter, melted
2 cups all-purpose flour	3 tablespoons graham-cracker crumbs
Apricot Filling, page 19	Powdered sugar

In a medium bowl, beat together 1/2 cup butter and sour cream. Add flour, blending well to make a soft dough. Wrap and refrigerate several hours or overnight. Dough may be kept in refrigerator up to 1 week. To bake strudel, prepare Apricot Filling; stir in pecans and set aside. Preheat oven to 350F (175C). Lightly grease a baking sheet. Divide dough into 3 equal portions. On a lightly floured surface, roll each portion into a 14" x 7" rectangle. Brush each lightly with 2 teaspoons melted butter. Sprinkle each rectangle with 1 tablespoon graham-cracker crumbs. Spread each evenly with 1/3 of Apricot Filling to within 1/2 inch of edges. Roll up dough, jelly-roll fashion, from long side. Place rolls on greased baking sheet. With a sharp knife, cut crosswise into 1-inch pieces, but do not separate. Bake 35 to 40 minutes or until golden. Cut slices apart. Cool on racks. While warm, sift powdered sugar over tops. Makes about 42 (1-inch) cookies.

Variation

Jam Strudel Slices: Prepare dough as directed. Omit brushing dough rectangles with melted butter and sprinkling with graham-cracker crumbs. Omit Apricot Filling, spreading each dough rectangle instead with 1/3 of Jam Filling to within 1/2 inch of edges. To prepare Jam Filling, in a small bowl, combine 1 cup strawberry or raspberry jam, 1 cup flaked or shredded coconut and 1 cup finely chopped walnuts. Proceed as directed above.

Back to front: Three-In-One Cookies, Bon Bon version, page 115; Almond Meringues, page 43; Chocolate-Cherry Bon Bons, pages 98-99; Florentine Triangle Jewels, page 91; Marzipan Peaches, page 97; and Vienna Squares, page 95.

Russian Tea Cakes

Also known as Mexican wedding cakes, these rich tender cookies melt in your mouth.

1 cup butter, room temperature
1/2 cup powdered sugar
2 teaspoons vanilla extract
Pinch of salt

2 cups all-purpose flour
1/2 teaspoon baking soda
1 cup chopped pecans
Powdered sugar

Preheat oven to 350F (175C). In a large bowl, beat together butter, 1/2 cup powdered sugar, vanilla and salt until light and fluffy. Gradually beat in flour and baking soda until well blended. Stir in pecans. Drop dough by teaspoonfuls, 1-1/2 inches apart, on ungreased baking sheets. Or, roll dough by teaspoonfuls into balls or crescent shapes and place on ungreased baking sheets. Bake 13 to 15 minutes or until edges begin to brown lightly. Remove cookies from baking sheets; cool on racks. While warm, sift powdered sugar generously over tops. Makes 55 to 60 (1-1/2-inch) cookies.

Kourambiedes

These delicate butter cookies are traditional Greek fare.

1 cup unsalted butter, room temperature
1/3 cup powdered sugar
1 egg yolk
1-1/2 tablespoons brandy

1 teaspoon vanilla extract
2-1/2 cups cake flour
Powdered sugar

In a large bowl, beat butter with electric mixer at high speed until light-colored, about 10 minutes. Gradually beat in 1/3 cup powdered sugar until well blended. Beat in egg yolk, brandy and vanilla. Gradually beat in cake flour. Cover and refrigerate 1 hour. To bake cookies, preheat oven to 350F (175C). Shape dough into 1-inch balls. Place 1-1/2 inches apart on ungreased baking sheets. Bake 12 to 14 minutes or until bottoms are golden. Cookies should remain white on top. Remove cookies from baking sheets; cool on racks. While hot, sift powdered sugar generously over tops. Makes about 50 (1-1/2-inch) cookies.

Bullets

When we were growing up, my sister Tammie rated these her favorite cookies.

1/2 cup butter, room temperature
2 tablespoons granulated sugar
1 teaspoon vanilla extract
1 cup all-purpose flour

1 cup chopped black walnuts, walnuts or
    macadamia nuts
Powdered sugar

Preheat oven to 350F (175C). In a medium bowl, beat together butter, granulated sugar and vanilla until creamy. Add flour, beating until well blended. If necessary, work with fingers until dough holds together. Blend in nuts. Shape into 1-inch balls. Place 2 inches apart on ungreased baking sheets. Bake 15 to 17 minutes or until bottoms are golden. Remove cookies from baking sheets; cool on racks. While warm, roll in powdered sugar, coating completely. Makes 30 (1-1/2-inch) cookies.

Hungarian Kifli

Divine little cinnamon-nut-filled roll-ups. The dough is made with cottage cheese.

1 cup butter, room temperature
1 cup cream-style cottage cheese (8 oz.)

2 cups all-purpose flour
Cinnamon-Nut Filling, see below

Cinnamon-Nut Filling:
2 egg whites
2 cups finely chopped walnuts

1/2 cup sugar
2 tablespoons ground cinnamon

In a large bowl, beat together butter and cottage cheese until light and fluffy. Add flour, beating until dough forms a ball. Divide dough into 3 equal portions. Wrap and refrigerate until firm, several hours or overnight. To bake cookies, prepare Cinnamon-Nut Filling; set aside. Preheat oven to 375F (190C). Grease baking sheets. On a floured surface, roll dough, 1 portion at a time, into a 10-inch circle. Spread each circle with 1/3 of Cinnamon-Nut Filling to within 1/2 inch of edges. Cut each circle into 24 pie-shaped wedges. Beginning at outer edge, roll up each wedge tightly. Place point-side down, 1-1/2 inches apart, on greased baking sheets. Bake 13 to 15 minutes or until golden. Watch carefully. Remove cookies from baking sheets; cool on racks. Makes 72 (2" x 1-1/2") cookies.

Cinnamon-Nut Filling:
In a medium bowl, combine unbeaten egg whites, walnuts, sugar and cinnamon, blending well.

Berlinerkranser

Wreath-shape Norwegian holiday favorites.

1 cup butter or margarine,
   room temperature
3/4 cup powdered sugar
2 hard-cooked egg yolks, mashed
2 uncooked egg yolks

1 teaspoon vanilla extract
2-1/4 cups all-purpose flour
1 egg white, beaten slightly
Red or green sugar crystals
12 red candied cherries, cut in quarters

In a large bowl, beat together butter or margarine, powdered sugar, egg yolks and vanilla until fluffy. Add flour, beating until blended. Wrap and refrigerate at least 2 hours. Allow dough to stand at room temperature until pliable enough to handle easily. To bake cookies, preheat oven to 350F (175C). Divide dough into 2 equal portions. Cut each portion into 24 equal pieces. On a piece of waxed paper, roll each piece of dough into a 5-inch-long rope. On ungreased baking sheets, shape each rope into a wreath or loop, overlapping both ends and allowing each end to extend 1/2 inch. Ropes should be 1-1/2 inches apart. Brush with egg white and sprinkle with colored sugar. Place a candied-cherry piece at top of each wreath, pressing in lightly. Bake 9 to 11 minutes or until edges are golden. Remove cookies from baking sheets; cool on racks. Makes 48 (1-3/4-inch) cookies.

Tip *Follow recipes exactly the first time around. After that, improvise to suit your tastes, if desired.*

Masterplan & Mix Cookies

When you want to make a batch of cookies in a hurry, start with a mix or a masterplan dough that can be used for an array of different creations. Some bakers use this to build a quick, vast cookie repertoire. Cookies made from a mix are often long on homemade taste, but short on last-minute work.

The mix might be a package of cake mix, pie-crust mix, a pie-crust stick or even a pudding mix that is speedily transformed into a cookie creation. It's amazing what you can produce from a package mix.

If a chocolate-and-caramel combination is one of your weaknesses, the fabulous layered Chocolate-Caramel Yummies made with a package of cake mix are a must. Refrigerator-style Devilish Mint Cookies are a tradition in our family.

If you opt for cookies made from a masterplan, two choices are offered—masterplan dough or a homemade masterplan dry cookie mix.

The dough can be kept on hand in the refrigerator up to a week. Or it can be frozen six to eight weeks to prepare a fresh batch of cookies speedily when the mood strikes. The homemade dry cookie mix can be stored eight to ten weeks in a tightly covered container on your pantry shelf. Even the kids can use the mastermix. With a few simple additions, the dough is ready to bake in a matter of minutes. Some of my favorites are Peanut-Butter Crisscrosses, Chocolate-Chip Brickles, Prune Squares, Orange Drops, Pineapple-Sour-Cream Cookies or Split-Layer Squares.

From one almond-paste-inspired dough, you can create variations by adding different ingredients and shaping the dough in different ways.

Wondering what you can do with Peanut-Butter Cutouts dough? Once you've tried the cutout cookies, why not bake Peanut-Butter & Chocolate Go-Rounds or Almost-Candy Cookies. The kids will be in heaven, nibbling on them.

If baking with mixes or using a masterplan appeals to you, the collection that follows should provide inspirations designed to make cookie baking simpler, faster and hopefully more efficient.

Fruited Cream-Cheese Gems

Whip these together in nothing flat using a package of yellow-cake mix.

1/4 cup butter or margarine,
    room temperature
1 (8-oz.) pkg. cream cheese,
    room temperature
1 egg yolk
1 teaspoon vanilla extract

1 (18.5-oz.) pkg. yellow-cake mix
1 cup raisins, chopped pitted dates or
    chopped dried apricots
1/3 cup flaked or shredded coconut
1/2 cup chopped walnuts

Preheat oven to 350F (175C). Grease a baking sheet. In a large bowl, beat together butter or margarine, cream cheese, egg yolk and vanilla until creamy. Beat in dry cake mix, 1/3 at a time, blending in last portion by hand. Stir in raisins, dates or apricots, coconut and walnuts. Drop by level tablespoonfuls, 2 inches apart, on greased baking sheets. Bake 13 to 15 minutes or until lightly browned. Remove cookies from baking sheets; cool on racks. Makes about 48 (1-3/4-inch) cookies.

Coffee-Toffee Bars

Rich and fabulous—similar to a pie made famous by a San Francisco confectioner.

1 stick pie-crust mix
1 oz. unsweetened chocolate, grated
1/4 cup packed brown sugar
3/4 cup finely chopped walnuts

1 tablespoon cold water
1 teaspoon vanilla extract
Coffee-Cream Filling, see below
Chocolate Topping, see below

Coffee-Cream Filling:
1/4 cup butter, room temperature
1 cup powdered sugar

1/4 cup whipping cream
2 teaspoons instant-coffee powder

Chocolate Topping:
1 cup (6 oz.) semisweet chocolate pieces
2 tablespoons butter

2 teaspoons light corn syrup

Preheat oven to 375F (190C). Line an 11" x 7" baking pan with foil. In a small bowl, crumble pie-crust mix. Stir in grated chocolate, brown sugar and walnuts. Drizzle water and vanilla over mixture. Toss with fork until thoroughly blended. Mixture will be crumbly. Press mixture evenly in bottom of foil-lined baking pan. Bake 13 to 15 minutes or until lightly browned. Cool in pan. Prepare Coffee-Cream Filling; spread over cooled crust. Refrigerate until filling is firm, about 30 minutes. Prepare Chocolate Topping; cool slightly. Spread Chocolate Topping evenly over filling. Refrigerate in pan. Cut chilled cookies into squares. Store in refrigerator. Makes 32 (1-3/4" x 1-1/2") cookies.

Coffee-Cream Filling:
In a medium bowl, use an electric mixer to beat together butter, powdered sugar, whipping cream and coffee powder until fluffy.

Chocolate Topping:
In top of a double boiler, combine chocolate pieces and butter. Heat over hot but not boiling water until melted and smooth, stirring occasionally. Stir in corn syrup.

Easy-As-Pie Chocolate-Chip Squares

Quick and easy when you need a fast treat.

1/4 cup butter or margarine,
  room temperature
3/4 cup granulated sugar
3 eggs
1 teaspoon vanilla extract
1/2 cup raisins

3/4 cup (4-1/2 oz.) semisweet chocolate
  pieces
1 cup chopped walnuts
1 stick pie-crust mix
Powdered sugar

Preheat oven to 325F (165C). Grease an 8- or 9-inch-square baking pan. In a medium bowl, beat together butter or margarine and granulated sugar until creamy. Beat in eggs and vanilla. Mixture may look slightly curdled. Stir in raisins, chocolate pieces and walnuts. Crumble in pie-crust mix, stirring with a fork until well blended. Spread evenly in greased baking pan. Bake 35 to 40 minutes or until set. Cool in pan. Sift powdered sugar over top. Cut cooled cookies into squares. Makes 25 (1-1/2-inch) cookies.

Surprise Chocolate Balls

They'll never guess pie-crust mix is used in these cookies!

1 cup (6 oz.) semisweet chocolate pieces
1 (11-oz.) pkg. pie-crust mix
1 teaspoon vanilla extract
1 to 1-1/2 teaspoons rum extract

3/4 cup finely chopped walnuts
3/4 cup unsweetened cocoa
1 cup powdered sugar

Preheat oven to 400F (205C). In top of a double boiler, melt chocolate over hot but not boiling water. Remove pan from water. Gradually stir in half the pie-crust mix, vanilla and rum extract, blending well. Stir in remaining pie-crust mix until blended. Stir in walnuts. Shape dough into 1-inch balls. Place 1-1/2 inches apart on ungreased baking sheets. Bake 10 minutes. In a medium bowl, sift together cocoa and powdered sugar. Cool cookies 5 minutes on baking sheets; then carefully roll each cookie in cocoa-sugar mixture. Cool on racks. When cool, roll in cocoa-sugar mixture again. Store cookies in remaining cocoa mixture in covered container. Makes 50 to 60 (1-1/4-inch) cookies.

Lemon-Toffee Balls

Lemon pudding and pie filling blend with candy to make these interesting butter-rich balls.

1 cup butter, room temperature
1/3 cup powdered sugar
1 (3-oz.) pkg. lemon-pudding and
  pie-filling mix
2 teaspoons water
1 teaspoon vanilla extract

2 cups all-purpose flour
1 cup chopped pecans
2 (1-1/16-oz.) pkgs. (containing 2 bars each)
  chocolate-coated English toffee candy,
  crushed
Powdered sugar, if desired

Preheat oven to 325F (165C). In a large bowl, beat together butter, 1/3 cup powdered sugar, pudding and pie-filling mix, water, vanilla and flour until dough forms. Stir in pecans and crushed candy, blending well. Shape into 1-inch balls. Place 1-1/2 inches apart on ungreased baking sheets. Bake 15 minutes or until golden. Cool on baking sheets. Sift powdered sugar over tops, if desired. Makes about 64 (1-3/8-inch) cookies.

Butter-Brickle Cookies

Cake mix is the base for these refrigerator-style cookies. Keep some handy to bake on short notice.

1 (18.5-oz.) pkg. yellow-cake mix	**1 (6-oz.) pkg. almond-brickle chips**
1 egg	**3/4 cup finely chopped pecans**
1/2 cup butter or margarine, melted, cooled	

In a medium bowl, combine cake mix, egg and butter or margarine, blending well by hand. Add brickle chips and pecans, blending well. Divide dough into 2 equal portions. Shape each portion into a log 10 inches long and 1-1/2 to 1-3/4 inches in diameter. Wrap and refrigerate until firm, several hours or overnight. To bake cookies, preheat oven to 300F (150C). Lightly grease baking sheets. Cut chilled dough into 1/4-inch slices. Place about 1 inch apart on greased baking sheets. Bake 9 to 11 minutes or until edges are very lightly browned. Do not overbake. Remove cookies from baking sheets; cool on racks. Makes about 72 (1-3/4-inch) cookies.

Devilish Mint Cookies

In these crisp family favorites, the mystery ingredient is cake mix.

1 (18.5-oz.) pkg. devil's-food-cake mix	**1/2 teaspoon peppermint extract**
1 egg	**1 cup (6 oz.) semisweet chocolate pieces**
3 tablespoons water	**3/4 cup chopped walnuts**

In a large bowl, combine cake mix, egg, water and peppermint extract until mixture is thoroughly blended and forms a dough mass. Stir in chocolate pieces and walnuts. Divide dough into 3 equal portions. Shape each portion into a log 9 inches long and 1-1/2 inches in diameter. Wrap and freeze until firm, at least 1 to 2 hours. To bake cookies, preheat oven to 350F (175C). Grease baking sheets. Using a sharp knife, cut frozen dough into 1/4-inch slices. Place 1 inch apart on greased baking sheets. Bake 11 to 12 minutes or until bottoms are lightly browned. Remove cookies from baking sheets; cool on racks. Makes 90 to 95 (2-inch) cookies.

Chocolate-Caramel Yummies

These freeze well and taste great partially frozen.

1 (14-oz.) pkg. vanilla caramels, unwrapped	**1 cup chopped walnuts**
1 (5.33-oz.) can evaporated milk (2/3 cup)	**3/4 cup butter or margarine, melted**
1 (18.5-oz.) pkg. German-chocolate- or devil's-food-cake mix	**1 cup (6 oz.) semisweet chocolate pieces**

Preheat oven to 350F (175C). Grease a 13" x 9" baking pan. In a medium saucepan, combine caramels and 1/3 cup evaporated milk. Heat over low heat until melted and smooth, stirring frequently; set aside. In a large bowl, combine cake mix, walnuts, remaining evaporated milk and melted butter or margarine until blended. Press half the cake mixture evenly in bottom of greased baking pan. Bake 6 minutes. Remove from oven; sprinkle with chocolate pieces. Let stand a few minutes or until melted. Carefully spread chocolate over crust. Cool slightly; then carefully spread warm caramel mixture evenly over chocolate. Drop remaining cake mixture by spoonfuls over caramel mixture; spread evenly. Bake 15 to 18 minutes or until edges begin to brown lightly. Cool slightly in pan. Refrigerate 1 hour or longer to set caramel mixture. Cut chilled cookies into squares. Makes about 48 (1-1/2-inch) cookies.

How to Make Master Cookie Mix

1/In a large bowl, beat together ingredients until mixture resembles coarse meal.

2/Store mix in a large airtight container. Label and store in a cool, dry place.

Master Cookie Mix   *Photo on page 113.*

A versatile mix to keep on your pantry shelf for making cookies in a hurry.

4 cups vegetable shortening
2 cups granulated sugar
2 cups packed brown sugar
8-1/2 cups all-purpose flour

2 cups instant-milk powder
3-1/2 tablespoons baking powder
2 teaspoons salt

In an extra-large bowl, beat together shortening, granulated sugar and brown sugar until light and fluffy. Gradually add flour, milk powder, baking powder and salt, blending well with electric mixer or pastry blender. Mixture will resemble coarse meal. Put in a large airtight container. Label and store in a cool, dry place. Use within 8 to 10 weeks. Makes about 18 cups Master Cookie Mix.

Master Cookie Mix can be used to make Peanut-Butter Crisscrosses, page 112; Chocolate-Chip Brickles, opposite; Prune Squares, page 112; Orange Drops, page 112; Pineapple-Sour-Cream Cookies, opposite; and Split-Layer Squares, opposite.

Split-Layer Squares

Easily prepared with Master Cookie Mix from your pantry shelf.

2 cups Master Cookie Mix, opposite
2 tablespoons water
1/2 cup packed brown sugar
2 tablespoons all-purpose flour
1/4 teaspoon baking powder

1/2 teaspoon vanilla extract
1 egg
3/4 cup (4-1/2 oz.) semisweet chocolate
  pieces
1/2 cup chopped walnuts

Preheat oven to 350F (175C). Grease an 8-inch-square baking pan. In a medium bowl, combine Master Cookie Mix and water until blended. Press mixture evenly into bottom of greased baking pan. Bake 10 minutes. Meanwhile, in a medium bowl, combine brown sugar, flour, baking powder, vanilla and egg until blended. Stir in chocolate pieces. Spoon evenly over hot crust, spreading evenly. Sprinkle with walnuts. Bake 25 to 30 minutes or until golden and cooked through. Cool in pan. Cut cooled cookies into squares. Makes 25 (1-1/2-inch) cookies.

Chocolate-Chip Brickles

Fast and easy—flavored with almond-brickle chips and chocolate pieces.

3 cups Master Cookie Mix, opposite
3 tablespoons packed brown sugar
1 egg

1-1/2 teaspoons vanilla extract
1 cup (6 oz.) semisweet chocolate pieces
1 (6-oz.) pkg. almond-brickle chips

Preheat oven to 375F (190C). In a large bowl, combine Master Cookie Mix, brown sugar, egg and vanilla until blended. Stir in chocolate pieces and almond-brickle chips. Drop by teaspoonfuls, 2 inches apart, on ungreased baking sheets. Bake 9 to 11 minutes or until edges are browned. Remove cookies from baking sheets; cool on racks. Makes about 55 (2-inch) cookies.

Pineapple-Sour-Cream Cookies

Moist and delicate.

3 cups Master Cookie Mix, opposite
1 (8-oz.) can juice-pack crushed pineapple

1/3 cup dairy sour cream

Preheat oven to 350F (175C). Grease baking sheets. In a medium bowl, combine Master Cookie Mix, undrained crushed pineapple and sour cream until blended. Drop by teaspoonfuls, 2 inches apart, on greased baking sheets. Bake 11 to 12 minutes or until bottoms are golden. Remove cookies from baking sheets; cool on racks. Makes about 45 (2-inch) cookies.

Tip

Most cookies will keep 3 to 4 days, even up to a week, at room temperature. For longer storage, freezing is advisable.

Peanut-Butter Crisscrosses

Good old-fashioned flavor.

3 cups Master Cookie Mix, page 110
3/4 cup smooth or crunchy peanut butter
1/3 cup packed brown sugar

1 egg
1 teaspoon vanilla extract

Preheat oven to 375F (190C). In a large bowl, combine Master Cookie Mix, peanut butter, brown sugar, egg and vanilla until blended. Shape into 1-inch balls. Place 2 inches apart on ungreased baking sheets; flatten with a fork in a crisscross pattern. Bake 10 to 12 minutes or until golden. Remove from baking sheets; cool on racks. Makes about 60 (2-inch) cookies.

Prune Squares

An uncooked prune filling is layered between cinnamon dough flavored with coconut and nuts.

1 (8-oz.) pkg. pitted prunes
1/3 cup orange juice
1-1/2 cups Master Cookie Mix, page 110
3/4 teaspoon ground cinnamon

3/4 cup flaked or shredded coconut
3/4 cup chopped walnuts
1 tablespoon water

Preheat oven to 350F (175C). Grease an 8-inch-square baking pan. In a food processor fitted with a steel blade, combine prunes and orange juice. Process until prunes are very fine; set aside. In a medium bowl, combine Master Cookie Mix, cinnamon, coconut and walnuts. Remove 1 cup; set aside. To mixture remaining in bowl, add water, stirring until blended. Press mixture evenly in bottom of greased baking pan. Spread evenly with prune mixture. Sprinkle with remaining crumb mixture, pressing in lightly. Bake 30 to 35 minutes or until top is golden brown. Cool in pan. Cut cooled cookies into squares. Makes about 25 (1-1/2-inch) cookies.

Orange Drops

Flavorful with orange peel and juice.

2 cups Master Cookie Mix, page 110
1 egg
1 tablespoon orange juice
1 tablespoon grated orange peel
1/2 cup chopped walnuts, if desired

1/3 cup flaked or shredded coconut,
 if desired
Orange Icing, see below
1/4 cup freshly grated orange peel

Orange Icing:
6 tablespoons butter, melted
1-1/2 cups powdered sugar

5 to 6 teaspoons orange juice

Preheat oven to 375F (190C). In a medium bowl, combine Master Cookie Mix, egg, orange juice, 1 tablespoon orange peel, and walnuts and coconut, if desired. Drop by teaspoonfuls, 2 inches apart, on ungreased baking sheets. Bake 10 minutes or until edges begin to brown. Remove from baking sheets; cool on racks. Prepare Orange Icing. Spread cooled cookies with icing. Garnish with 1/4 cup orange peel. Makes about 30 (2-inch) cookies.

Orange Icing:
In a medium bowl, stir sugar in hot butter. Add juice, one teaspoon at a time, until desired consistency is achieved.

Back to front: Master Cookie Mix, page 110; Peanut-Butter Crisscrosses, Orange Drops, and Prune Squares, above.

How to Make Three-In-One Cookies

1/To make Nutty Wafers, cut logs into 1/4-inch slices. Place on greased baking sheets. Top each with a candied-cherry half.

2/To make Bon Bons, frost tops of cooled cookies with Bon-Bon Icing, tinted to color of your choice.

3/To make Checkerboard Cookies, shape each dough portion into 4 logs 15 inches long and 1/2 inch in diameter.

4/Press logs together to form a checkerboard pattern. Wrap and refrigerate. Cut logs into 1/4-inch slices.

Three-In-One Cookies

Make Nutty Wafers, Bon Bons and Checkerboard Cookies from this basic dough.

1 cup butter or margarine, room temperature
1/2 cup sugar
1 egg yolk
1 tablespoon grated orange peel
1 teaspoon vanilla extract
2-1/2 cups all-purpose flour

In a large bowl, beat together butter or margarine, sugar, egg yolk, orange peel and vanilla until light and fluffy. Add flour, beating until blended. Divide dough into 2 equal portions. Each portion equals 1/2 recipe. Shape in any of the 3 ways described below, chilling if necessary. Preheat oven to 350F (175C). Grease baking sheets. Bake as directed below.

Nutty Wafers:
Shape 1/2 recipe dough (1 portion) into 2 logs, 8-1/2 inches long and 1 inch in diameter. Roll each log in 3 tablespoons finely chopped walnuts or pecans. Wrap and refrigerate until firm, at least 2 hours. To bake, cut chilled dough into 1/4-inch slices. Place 1 inch apart on greased baking sheets. Press a semisweet chocolate piece or half of a red or green candied cherry into top of each cookie. Bake 10 to 12 minutes or until bottoms are golden. Remove cookies from baking sheets; cool on racks. Makes 55 to 60 (1-1/4-inch) cookies.

Bon Bons: *Photo on page 103.*
Using 1/2 recipe dough (1 portion), wrap 1-1/2 teaspoons dough around a pecan half or a drained maraschino-cherry half. Place 1-1/2 inches apart on greased baking sheets. Bake 10 to 12 minutes or until bottoms are golden. Remove cookies from baking sheets; cool on racks. Frost tops of cooled cookies with Bon-Bon Icing. Allow to stand until set. To make Bon-Bon Icing, in a small bowl, beat together 2 tablespoons room-temperature butter, 2 tablespoons whipping cream or milk, 1 teaspoon vanilla extract and 1 cup powdered sugar until smooth. Blend in a few drops yellow or red food coloring, if desired. Makes 30 (1-1/2-inch) cookies.

Checkerboard Cookies:
Use 1 recipe dough (2 portions). To 1 portion add 2 ounces melted unsweetened chocolate, blending well. Leave other portion plain. Shape chocolate dough into 4 logs 15 inches long and 1/2 inch in diameter. Shape plain dough into 4 logs, each 15 inches long and 1/2 inch in diameter. Place 1 chocolate log next to 1 plain log; then place a plain log on top of chocolate log and a chocolate log on top of plain log to form a checkerboard pattern. Press together lightly to form a compact log. Repeat with remaining dough logs. Cut each log in half for ease in handling. Wrap and refrigerate until firm, at least 2 hours. Cut chilled dough into 1/4-inch slices. Place 1 inch apart on greased baking sheets. Bake 8 to 10 minutes or until plain dough is golden. Remove cookies from baking sheets; cool on racks. Makes about 115 (1-1/2-inch) cookies.

 **Tip**
Avoid using dark baking sheets. They absorb heat and cause uneven browning and overbrowning. A shiny baking sheet is recommended for delicate browning.

Peanut-Butter-Cookie Cutouts

This soft dough requires care in handling.

1/2 cup butter or margarine,
   room temperature
1/2 cup smooth peanut butter
3/4 cup packed brown sugar
1 egg

1 teaspoon vanilla extract
4 teaspoons grated orange peel, if desired
1-1/2 cups all-purpose flour
1/2 teaspoon baking soda

In a medium bowl, beat together butter or margarine, peanut butter, brown sugar, egg, vanilla and orange peel, if desired, until light and fluffy. Add flour and baking soda, beating until blended. Wrap and refrigerate until firm, 2 to 3 hours. To bake cookies, preheat oven to 350F (175C). Grease baking sheets. On a floured surface, roll dough 3/16 inch thick. With lightly floured cookie cutters, cut into desired shapes. Place 1 inch apart on greased baking sheets. Bake 10 to 12 minutes or until golden. Do not overbake. Remove cookies from baking sheets; cool on racks. Makes about 30 (2-3/4-inch) cookies.

Variations

Dough can also be used to make Almost-Candy Cookies, page 136; Peanut-Butter & Chocolate Go-Rounds, page 49; and Peanut-Butter & Jelly Sandwiches, page 125.

Cream-Cheese Pastry

A versatile pastry dough used to make Rugelach, page 71, Chocolate-Pecan Tassies, page 102.

1 (8-oz.) pkg. cream cheese,
   room temperature
1 cup butter, room temperature

2 teaspoons vanilla extract
2 cups all-purpose flour

In a food processor fitted with a steel blade, process cream cheese, butter and vanilla until smooth. Add flour; process until well blended and dough begins to cling together in a ball. Use immediately as recipe directs or wrap and store. May be stored in refrigerator up to 1 week. May be frozen, wrapped airtight, in moisture- and vapor-proof paper up to 2 months. Thaw in refrigerator several hours before using. Use to make Rugelach, page 71, or Chocolate-Pecan Tassies, page 102.

Tip *It is not necessary to wash baking sheets between cookie batches. Wipe off sheets with a greased paper towel if sheet is to be greased, brushing away any crumbs.*

Basic Almond-Paste Cookie Dough

This versatile dough can be used to make your choice of three different cookies.

2 (7-oz.) pkgs. almond paste, room temperature
2 cups butter, room temperature
1-3/4 cups sugar
3 eggs

2 teaspoons vanilla extract
5-3/4 cups all-purpose flour
1/4 teaspoon salt

In a large bowl, crumble almond paste with your fingers. Add butter, beating with electric mixer until smooth. With mixer on medium speed, beat in sugar, eggs and vanilla, until light and fluffy. Gradually add flour and salt, beating until thoroughly blended. Divide dough into 4 equal portions. Each portion equals 1/4 recipe. Shape each portion into a 6-inch-diameter disk. Use dough immediately as recipe directs or wrap and refrigerate at least 1 hour. Use 1/4 recipe of dough to make each of the following cookies: Linzer Squares, page 28; Chocolate-Cherry Bon Bons, page 98; and Marzipan Peaches, page 97.

Basic Butter-Cookie Dough

Three kinds of cookies can be made using this dough.

1 cup butter or margarine, room temperature
3/4 cup sugar
1 egg

1 teaspoon vanilla extract
2-1/2 cups all-purpose flour
1 teaspoon baking powder

In a medium bowl, beat together butter or margarine, sugar, egg and vanilla until light and fluffy. Add flour and baking powder, beating until blended. Use dough immediately as recipe directs or wrap and store. May be stored in refrigerator up to 1 week. May be frozen, wrapped airtight, in moisture- and vapor-proof paper up to 2 months. Thaw in refrigerator several hours before using. Use dough to make Chocolate-Peppermint Bites, page 63; Two-Tone Cookie Roll, page 50; and Cookie Candy Canes, page 75.

Tip *For fun, design your own cookie patterns from cardboard. Children's books and children's drawings provide excellent ideas. To keep the pattern from slipping off the dough while cutting, grease one side of the pattern. Place greased-side down on dough.*

Lunch Box & Travel Cookies

Kids crave cookies as lunch-box desserts, after-school snacks or anytime they can get their hands on them. After all, what would childhood be without snatching a favorite cookie now and then?

When faced with the brown-bag brigade, make the cookies you pack interesting and creative. Don't be limited to the same old goodies. There are numerous cookie possibilities as you'll see when you glance at this section.

Keep these recipes in mind for packing on picnics, hikes, bicycle rides, camp-outs and other outdoor occasions.

Although cookies or desserts are optional and not the mainstay of the lunch routine, children expect them, especially if they don't need to count calories. Make them as healthful as possible by including oatmeal, raisins, wheat germ, peanut butter, sunflower nuts, dried fruit or cereals. Use cookies as a vehicle to introduce your children to ingredients they might not otherwise want to sample.

To help take the drudgery out of the daily lunch-making task, have a baking session. Prepare enough cookies for a week or a month at a time and keep a variety handy in the freezer. If you have the time, recruit the children to help make their own lunch-box treats. They'll take special pride in their cookie achievements, especially when it comes time to enjoy their efforts at school. But before you settle on which ones to make, consult your children about their cookie likes and dislikes. Otherwise, your efforts may end up being traded-away at lunch time.

Chewy Fruit Bars with their wonderful spicy flavor are excellent travelers and keepers. Vary the fruit—use raisins or dried apricots and pitted dates or prunes. If you really like fig bars, make a batch of Whole-Wheat Fig Bars.

If you are a whole-wheat buff, bake Whole-Wheat Chippers. If brown-baggers are partial to crunchy, chewy cookies, give them Honey Crunchies, prepared with two kinds of cereal and coconut.

Cookies are the way to a child's heart. Make their snacks as healthful as possible. No generation should grow up without an ample supply of mom's delicious home-baked delights.

Choco-Nut Delights

During college, a friend's care package from home was always filled with these tasty treats.

1/2 cup butter or margarine,
   room temperature
1/2 cup packed brown sugar
1/4 cup granulated sugar
1 egg
1-1/2 teaspoons vanilla extract
1-1/4 cups all-purpose flour

1/2 teaspoon baking soda
1/4 teaspoon salt
2 cups (12 oz.) semisweet chocolate pieces
1/3 cup maple syrup
2 tablespoons butter or margarine
Pinch of salt
2 cups chopped pecans

Preheat oven to 350F (175C). In a medium bowl, beat together 1/2 cup butter or margarine, brown sugar, granulated sugar, egg and 1/2 teaspoon vanilla until light and fluffy. Add flour, baking soda and 1/4 teaspoon salt. Spread evenly in bottom of an ungreased 13" x 9" baking pan. Bake 15 to 18 minutes or until light golden. Sprinkle immediately with 1 cup chocolate pieces. Let stand 2 minutes or until melted. Spread chocolate evenly over crust. In top of a double boiler, combine remaining 1 cup chocolate pieces, maple syrup, 2 tablespoons butter or margarine, remaining 1 teaspoon vanilla and pinch of salt. Heat over hot but not boiling water until melted and smooth, stirring occasionally. Stir in pecans. Spread evenly over chocolate. Bake 8 minutes. Cool in pan. Cut cooled cookies into bars. Makes 40 (1-3/4" x 1-1/2") cookies.

Saucepan Applesauce Bars

A quick-to-fix, cake-like bar, made in a saucepan.

1/3 cup butter or margarine
1 cup packed brown sugar
1/2 cup unsweetened applesauce
1 egg
1 teaspoon vanilla extract
Pinch of salt
1-1/4 cups all-purpose flour

1 teaspoon baking powder
1/4 teaspoon baking soda
3/4 teaspoon ground cinnamon
1/4 teaspoon ground nutmeg
1/2 cup raisins
2/3 cup chopped walnuts
1/2 recipe Orange Glaze, page 120

Preheat oven to 350F (175C). Grease a 13" x 9" baking pan. In a medium saucepan, melt butter or margarine over low heat. Remove from heat. Stir in brown sugar, applesauce, egg, vanilla and salt, blending well. Add flour, baking powder, baking soda, cinnamon and nutmeg, blending well. Stir in raisins and walnuts. Spread evenly in greased baking pan. Bake 23 to 25 minutes or until a wooden pick inserted in center comes out clean. Cool in pan. Meanwhile, prepare Orange Glaze. While warm, spread cookies with Orange Glaze. When glaze has set, cut into bars. Makes 40 (1-3/4" x 1-1/2") cookies.

Apple Snack Squares

A not-so-sweet choice for morning or afternoon snack break with milk or coffee.

1/3 cup butter or margarine
1/2 cup packed brown sugar
1 egg
1 teaspoon vanilla extract
1/2 cup all-purpose flour
1/2 cup whole-wheat flour

1 teaspoon baking powder
Pinch of salt
3/4 cup chopped unpeeled raw apple
1/2 cup sunflower nuts or chopped walnuts
Powdered sugar, if desired

Preheat oven to 350F (175C). Grease an 8- or 9-inch-square baking pan. In a medium saucepan, melt butter or margarine. Remove from heat; stir in brown sugar, egg and vanilla. Add all-purpose flour, whole-wheat flour, baking powder and salt, blending well. Stir in apple and sunflower nuts or walnuts. Spread dough evenly in greased baking pan. Bake 25 minutes. Cool in pan. Cut cooled cookies into squares. Sift powdered sugar over top, if desired. Makes 25 (1-1/2-inch) cookies.

Banana-Oatmeal Cookies

Bursting with bananas, oats, dates and sunflower nuts; frost with an orange glaze.

1/2 cup butter or margarine,
   room temperature
1/3 cup honey
2 eggs
1 cup mashed bananas (about 3 medium)
2 tablespoons grated orange peel
3/4 cup all-purpose flour
3/4 cup whole-wheat flour

1 teaspoon baking soda
1/2 teaspoon ground nutmeg
1-1/2 cups rolled oats
1/2 cup sunflower nuts
1/2 cup chopped pitted dates
Granulated sugar
Orange Glaze, see below

Orange Glaze:
1-1/2 cups powdered sugar
2 tablespoons butter or margarine,
   room temperature

2 to 2-1/2 tablespoons orange juice

In a large bowl, beat together butter or margarine, honey and eggs until light and fluffy. Stir in bananas and orange peel. Add all-purpose flour, whole-wheat flour, baking soda and nutmeg, beating until blended. Stir in oats, sunflower nuts and dates. Cover and refrigerate at least 1 hour. To bake cookies, preheat oven to 375F (190C). Lightly grease baking sheets. Drop dough by heaping teaspoonfuls, 1-1/2 inches apart, on greased baking sheets. Using bottom of glass dipped in granulated sugar, flatten cookies slightly. Bake 10 to 12 minutes or until edges are brown. Remove cookies from baking sheets; cool on racks. Meanwhile, prepare Orange Glaze. While cookies are warm, spread tops with Orange Glaze. Makes about 54 (2-1/4-inch) cookies.

Orange Glaze:
In a small bowl, combine powdered sugar, butter or margarine and orange juice until smooth and of spreading consistency.

Grandma's Raisin-Toffee Squares

Wholesome and delicious glazed cereal bars were my grandmother's favorites.

1/2 cup butter or margarine,
    room temperature
3/4 cup packed brown sugar
1 teaspoon vanilla extract
2 eggs

1 cup all-purpose flour
1 cup whole-bran cereal
1 cup raisins
Powdered-Sugar Icing, see below

Powdered-Sugar Icing:
1 cup powdered sugar
2 tablespoons butter or margarine,
    room temperature

1/2 teaspoon vanilla extract
1 to 2 tablespoons milk

Preheat oven to 350F (175C). Grease an 8- or 9-inch-square baking pan. In a medium bowl, beat together butter or margarine, brown sugar, vanilla and eggs until light and fluffy. Add flour, beating until blended. Stir in cereal and raisins. Spread evenly in greased baking pan. Bake 20 to 25 minutes or until a wooden pick inserted in center comes out clean. Cool in pan. Prepare Powdered-Sugar Icing. Spread cookies evenly with Powdered-Sugar Icing. When icing has set, cut into squares. Makes 25 (1-1/2-inch) cookies.

Powdered-Sugar Icing:
In a small bowl, combine powdered sugar, butter or margarine, vanilla and milk until smooth.

Chewy Fruit Bars

These hearty fruit bars store well—if they last that long!

1/3 cup vegetable shortening
1 cup sugar
1 egg
1/4 cup molasses
1/4 cup water
1/2 teaspoon vanilla extract
2 teaspoons ground cinnamon
1/4 teaspoon ground nutmeg

1/8 teaspoon ground mace
1/4 teaspoon salt
3 to 3-1/4 cups all-purpose flour
1/2 teaspoon baking soda
1 cup raisins or chopped dried apricots
1 cup chopped pitted dates or prunes
3/4 cup chopped walnuts
1 tablespoon evaporated milk

Preheat oven to 350F (175C). Grease 2 baking sheets. In a large bowl, beat together shortening, sugar and egg until creamy. Add molasses, water, vanilla, cinnamon, nutmeg, mace and salt, beating well. Add flour and baking soda, beating until blended. Stir in raisins or apricots, dates or prunes and walnuts. Refrigerate dough until no longer sticky, 1 hour or longer. Divide dough into 4 equal portions. Shape each portion into a log 14 inches long and 1 inch in diameter. Place 2 logs on each greased baking sheet. Pat each log down flat until each strip is 2 inches wide. Brush tops with evaporated milk. Bake 15 to 17 minutes or until golden. Cool 15 minutes on pan; then cut into 1-inch-diagonal pieces. Cool completely. Makes about 50 (1-inch) cookies.

Whole-Wheat Fig Bars

These become softer and more flavorful after standing at least a day.

1/3 cup vegetable shortening
1 cup packed brown sugar
2 eggs
1 teaspoon vanilla extract
1-1/4 cups all-purpose flour
1-1/4 cups whole-wheat flour

1/4 teaspoon baking soda
2 teaspoons baking powder
1 teaspoon grated orange peel
Pinch of salt
Fig Filling, see below

Fig Filling:

1 (8-oz.) pkg. dried figs, stems removed, chopped
2/3 cup water

3 tablespoons lemon or orange juice
3 tablespoons granulated sugar

In a large bowl, beat together shortening, brown sugar, eggs and vanilla until creamy. Add all-purpose flour, whole-wheat flour, baking soda, baking powder, orange peel and salt, beating until blended. Refrigerate dough 1 to 2 hours. Prepare Fig Filling; set aside. To bake cookies, preheat oven to 375F (190C). Grease baking sheets. On a floured surface, roll dough into a 14-inch square. Cut dough into 4 equal strips, each 14 inches long and 3-1/2 inches wide. Spoon 1/4 of Fig Filling in a 1-1/2-inch-wide mound down center of each strip. Using a long spatula, lift sides of each dough strip over filling, overlapping slightly on top. Press edges together to seal. Cut strips crosswise in half for ease in handling. Place, seam-side down, 3 inches apart on greased baking sheets. Brush off any excess flour. Cut each strip into 7 (1-inch) crosswise pieces, but do not separate. Bake 13 to 15 minutes or until puffed and firm to the touch. Cool 5 to 10 minutes on baking sheets; then cut apart and remove to racks to cool completely. Makes about 56 (2" x 1") cookies.

Fig Filling:
In a medium saucepan, combine figs, water, lemon or orange juice and granulated sugar. Bring to a boil over medium heat, stirring occasionally. Reduce heat and simmer 5 to 10 minutes or until thickened, stirring occasionally. Cool.

Whole-Wheat Chippers

Freeze a supply of these nutritious cookies to have on hand for lunch bags or snacks.

1/2 cup butter or margarine, room temperature
3/4 cup packed brown sugar
1 egg
1 teaspoon vanilla extract
1 cup whole-wheat flour

1/2 teaspoon baking soda
1/4 teaspoon salt
1 cup rolled oats
3/4 cup granola
1 cup (6 oz.) semisweet chocolate pieces

Preheat oven to 350F (175C). Grease baking sheets. In a medium bowl, beat together butter or margarine, brown sugar, egg and vanilla until light and fluffy. Add whole-wheat flour, baking soda and salt, beating well. Beat in oats and granola. Stir in chocolate pieces. Drop by teaspoonfuls, 2 inches apart, on greased baking sheets. Bake 10 minutes or until lightly browned. Remove cookies from baking sheets; cool on racks. Makes about 40 (1-3/4-inch) cookies.

How to Make Whole-Wheat Fig Bars

1/On a lightly floured surface, roll dough into a 14-inch square. Cut dough into 4 equal strips.

2/ Spoon 1/4 of Fig Filling in a 1-1/2-inch-wide mound down center of each strip.

3/Using a long spatula, lift sides of each dough strip over filling, overlapping slightly on top. Press to seal.

4/Cut each filled strip into 7 (1-inch) crosswise pieces, but do not separate.

Honey-Carrot Bars

Carrot-cake lovers will enjoy these moist nutritious bars.

1/3 cup vegetable oil
1/3 cup honey
2 eggs
1 teaspoon vanilla extract
1 cup whole-wheat flour
1 teaspoon baking powder
1 teaspoon baking soda

1-1/2 teaspoons ground cinnamon
3 tablespoons milk
1/2 cup well-drained crushed pineapple
1 cup finely shredded raw carrots
1/2 cup chopped walnuts
1/2 cup raisins
Cream-Cheese Frosting, see below

Cream-Cheese Frosting:
1 (3-oz.) pkg. cream cheese,
  room temperature
3 tablespoons butter or margarine,
  room temperature

1-1/4 cups powdered sugar
1 teaspoon vanilla extract
1 teaspoon grated orange peel

Preheat oven to 350F (175C). Grease a 13" x 9" baking pan. In a large bowl, combine oil, honey, eggs and vanilla. Add whole-wheat flour, baking powder, baking soda and cinnamon, stirring until blended. Stir in milk, pineapple, carrots, walnuts and raisins. Turn into greased baking pan. Bake 25 to 30 minutes or until a wooden pick inserted in center comes out clean. Cool in pan. Prepare Cream-Cheese Frosting. Spread cooled cookies with Cream-Cheese Frosting. Refrigerate. Cut chilled cookies into bars. Store in refrigerator. Makes 36 (2" x 1-1/2") cookies.

Cream-Cheese Frosting:
In a small bowl, beat together cream cheese, butter or margarine, powdered sugar, vanilla and orange peel until smooth.

Honey Crunchies

A crunchy and chewy cookie, great when traveling with children.

1 cup butter or margarine,
  room temperature
1/2 cup packed brown sugar
1/2 cup granulated sugar
1/2 cup honey
1 egg
2 cups all-purpose flour

1 teaspoon baking soda
1/2 teaspoon baking powder
Pinch of salt
2 cups toasted-corn-cereal flakes
2 cups oven-toasted-rice cereal
1 cup flaked or shredded coconut

Preheat oven to 375F (190C). In a large bowl, beat together butter or margarine, brown sugar, granulated sugar, honey and egg until creamy. Add flour, baking soda, baking powder and salt, beating until blended. Stir in cereals and coconut. Drop by teaspoonfuls, 2 inches apart, on ungreased baking sheets. Bake 8 to 10 minutes or until golden. Cool 2 to 3 minutes on baking sheets; then remove to racks to cool completely. Makes about 96 (2-inch) cookies.

Tip

When it comes to baking times, use a timer. DON'T GUESS.

Saucer Jumbos

Cookie monsters won't be able to resist these giants.

1/2 cup butter or margarine,
   room temperature
1/2 cup packed brown sugar
1/2 cup granulated sugar
1 egg
1 teaspoon vanilla extract
1/2 cup toasted wheat germ

3/4 cup all-purpose flour
1 teaspoon baking powder
1/4 teaspoon salt
1/2 cup rolled oats
1/4 cup flaked or shredded coconut
1/2 cup (3 oz.) semisweet chocolate pieces,
   raisins or peanut-butter-flavor pieces

Preheat oven to 375F (190C). Grease baking sheets. In a medium bowl, beat together butter or margarine, brown sugar, granulated sugar, egg and vanilla until light and fluffy. Add wheat germ, flour, baking powder, salt, oats and coconut, beating until blended. Stir in chocolate pieces, raisins or peanut-butter pieces. Drop dough by 1/4 cupfuls, about 6 inches apart, on greased baking sheets. Bake 15 to 17 minutes or until golden brown and centers are firm. Cool 2 to 3 minutes on baking sheets; then remove to racks to cool completely. Makes about 10 (4-inch) cookies.

Variation

For smaller cookies, drop dough by teaspoonfuls, 2 inches apart, on greased baking sheets. Bake 10 to 12 minutes or until golden. Makes about 48 (1-3/4-inch) cookies.

Peanut-Butter & Jelly Sandwiches

Team the kids' favorite flavors in these plain, tasty cookies.

1 recipe Peanut-Butter-Cookie Cutouts
   dough, page 116

1/3 cup strawberry jam or grape jelly,
   warmed if necessary

Divide Peanut-Butter-Cookie Cutouts dough into 2 equal portions. Shape each portion into a log 6 inches long and 2 inches in diameter. Wrap and freeze until firm, at least 1 hour. To bake cookies, preheat oven to 350F (175C). Cut frozen dough into 3/16-inch slices. Place 1 inch apart on ungreased baking sheets. Bake 8 to 10 minutes or until golden. Watch carefully. Remove cookies from baking sheets; cool on racks. Sandwich bottom sides of 2 cooled cookies together with jam or jelly between. Remove with remaining cookies. Makes about 32 (2-inch) filled cookies.

Variation

Peanut-Butter & Chocolate Sandwiches: Substitute 1/2 cup (3 ounces) semisweet chocolate pieces, melted, for jam or jelly. Sandwich bottom sides of 2 cooled cookies together with melted chocolate.

Cereal Chews

Butterscotch squares with moist coconut for extra chewiness.

1/3 cup butter or margarine
1/2 cup wheat and barley cereal,
   such as Grape-Nuts
3/4 cup packed brown sugar
1 egg

1 teaspoon vanilla extract
3/4 cup all-purpose flour
1/2 teaspoon baking powder
1/8 teaspoon baking soda
3/4 cup flaked or shredded coconut

Preheat oven to 350F (175C). Grease an 8-inch-square baking pan. In a medium saucepan, melt butter or margarine. Add cereal; cook 2 minutes, stirring constantly. Remove from heat. Stir in brown sugar. Stir in egg and vanilla until well blended. Add flour, baking powder and baking soda until well blended. Stir in coconut. Spread in greased baking pan. Bake 22 to 25 minutes or until golden. Cool in pan. While slightly warm, cut into squares. Makes 25 (1-1/2-inch) cookies.

Coconut-Oatmeal Crisps

When baking, allow plenty of space between these crispy cookies for spreading.

3/4 cup butter or margarine,
   room temperature
1 cup granulated sugar
1/2 cup packed brown sugar
2 eggs
2 teaspoons vanilla extract

1 cup all-purpose flour
1 teaspoon baking powder
1/2 teaspoon baking soda
Pinch of salt
1-1/4 cups flaked or shredded coconut
2-1/2 cups rolled oats

Preheat oven to 375F (190C). In a large bowl, beat together butter or margarine, granulated sugar, brown sugar, eggs and vanilla until fluffy. Add flour, baking powder, baking soda and salt, beating until blended. Stir in coconut and oats. Drop by teaspoonfuls, 3 inches apart, on ungreased baking sheets. Bake 10 to 12 minutes or until lightly browned. Cool 2 to 3 minutes on baking sheets; then remove to racks to cool completely. Makes about 65 (2-1/4-inch) cookies.

Oatmeal Jumbles

Coconut and granola add chewiness to these giant cookies.

1/2 cup butter or margarine,
   room temperature
3/4 cup granulated sugar
3/4 cup packed brown sugar
1 egg
1-1/2 teaspoons butter flavoring
1 teaspoon vanilla extract
1-1/4 cups all-purpose flour

1/2 teaspoon baking soda
1/2 teaspoon baking powder
3/4 cup rolled oats
3/4 cup granola
3/4 cup flaked or shredded coconut
1 cup (6 oz.) semisweet chocolate pieces or
   raisins

Preheat oven to 350F (175C). In a large bowl, beat together butter or margarine, granulated sugar, brown sugar, egg, butter flavoring and vanilla until light and fluffy. Add flour, baking soda and baking powder, beating until well blended. Stir in oats, granola, coconut and chocolate pieces or raisins. Shape dough into 1-3/4-inch balls. Place 3 inches apart on ungreased baking sheets. Bake 12 to 15 minutes or until golden brown. Cool 2 to 3 minutes on baking sheets; then remove to racks to cool completely. Makes about 20 (3-inch) cookies.

How to Make Crunchy Date Rounds

1/Drop dough by teaspoonfuls into crushed cereal; roll to coat completely.

2/Place 2 inches apart on baking sheets, flattening slightly with the bottom of a glass.

Crunchy Date Rounds

Crushed cereal flakes provide the crunch on these tasty treats.

1/4 cup vegetable shortening	**1-1/4 cups all-purpose flour**
1/4 cup butter or margarine,	**1/2 teaspoon baking soda**
room temperature	**1/4 teaspoon salt**
1/2 cup granulated sugar	**1/2 cup chopped walnuts**
1/4 cup packed brown sugar	**1/2 cup chopped pitted dates or raisins**
1 egg	**1-1/2 cups toasted-corn-cereal flakes,**
1 teaspoon vanilla extract	**coarsely crushed**

Preheat oven to 375F (190C). Grease baking sheets. In a large bowl, beat together shortening, butter or margarine, granulated sugar, brown sugar, egg and vanilla until light and fluffy. Add flour, baking soda and salt, beating until thoroughly blended. Stir in walnuts and dates or raisins. Drop dough by teaspoonfuls into crushed cereal; roll to coat completely. Place 2 inches apart on greased baking sheets, flattening slightly with the bottom of a glass. Bake 12 to 13 minutes or until golden. Remove cookies from baking sheets; cool on racks. Makes about 36 (2-1/4-inch) cookies.

Honey-Granola Bars

Packed with healthful ingredients, these are good to go in lunch boxes.

1/4 cup butter or margarine, room temperature	**3/4 cup all-purpose flour**
1/4 cup packed brown sugar	**1 teaspoon baking soda**
1/3 cup honey	**1/2 teaspoon ground cinnamon**
1 egg	**1 cup granola**
1 teaspoon vanilla extract	**1/4 cup toasted wheat germ**
2 tablespoons milk	**1/2 cup raisins**
Pinch of salt	**1/4 cup sunflower nuts**
	Powdered sugar, if desired

Preheat oven to 350F (175C). Grease a 13'' x 9'' baking pan generously. In a medium bowl, beat butter or margarine and brown sugar until creamy. Add honey, egg, vanilla, milk and salt. Beat in flour, baking soda and cinnamon until blended. Stir in granola, wheat germ, raisins and sunflower nuts. Spread dough in greased baking pan. Bake 15 to 20 minutes or until a wooden pick inserted in center comes out clean. Cool in pan. While slightly warm, cut into bars. Sift powdered sugar over top, if desired. Makes 36 (2-1/8'' x 1-1/2'') cookies.

Granola Cookies

A good choice for lunch boxes or after-school snacks.

1/2 cup vegetable shortening	**3/4 teaspoon baking soda**
1 cup packed brown sugar	**1/4 teaspoon salt**
1/3 cup instant-milk powder	**1/2 cup (3 oz.) semisweet chocolate pieces or** raisins
1 egg	
1-1/2 teaspoons vanilla extract	**1/2 cup flaked or shredded coconut**
3/4 cup all-purpose flour	**2 cups granola**

Preheat oven to 350F (175C). In a medium bowl, beat shortening, sugar, milk powder, egg and vanilla until fluffy. Add flour, baking soda and salt, beating until blended. Stir in chocolate pieces or raisins, coconut and granola. Shape dough into 1-1/4-inch balls. Place 2 inches apart on ungreased baking sheets. Bake 10 to 12 minutes or until lightly browned. Cool 1 to 2 minutes on baking sheets; remove to racks to cool completely. Makes about 45 (1-3/4-inch) cookies.

Brittle Squares

Crisp and buttery, chocolate-chip lovers are bound to go for these.

1 cup butter or margarine, room temperature	**2 cups all-purpose flour**
3/4 cup packed brown sugar	**1-1/2 cups chopped walnuts or pecans**
2 teaspoons vanilla extract	**1 cup (6 oz.) semisweet chocolate pieces**
1/4 teaspoon salt	

Preheat oven to 375F (190C). Line a 15'' x 10'' jelly-roll pan with foil. In a large bowl, beat together butter or margarine, brown sugar, vanilla and salt until creamy. Add flour, beating until well blended. Stir in nuts and chocolate pieces, blending well. Spread dough evenly in foil-lined jelly-roll pan. Bake 20 to 25 minutes or until lightly browned. Cool 2 to 3 minutes in pan; then cut into squares. Cool completely. Makes about 60 (1-1/2-inch) cookies.

Easy Enough for Kids

When young chefs in your house want to venture into the kitchen and prepare a cookie-treat, have them take a look at this selection of recipes. Some recipes are easy enough to be followed completely by a child, others will take some supervision.

For teenagers, a Cookie Pizza offers novel treatment of a delicious oatmeal-cookie dough. Topped with nuts and chocolate pieces, the creation is baked on a 12-inch pizza pan and served pizza-style, cut in wedges.

When mom doesn't have much time to get involved in cookie-making, try In-A-Hurry Gingerbread Cookies. They're simple to create with a package of gingerbread mix and warm water. Once chilled, roll and cut to your heart's content, using cookie cutters or your own designs. Remember that coloring books, free-hand drawings and magazines are good sources for pattern ideas. For fun, let each child draw a pattern of his or her own to cut and bake. Then frost and decorate as desired. This is a good last-minute idea when time is running out for holiday gifts. Or, you might even enjoy it as a Christmas-Eve project with the entire family participating.

If baking safety is a worry, let the kids stir together some no-bake sweets. Peanut-Butter-Candy Cookies are an indescribably good refrigerator confection. Orange-Fruit Balls are a good snack. They go together quickly and provide children with a feeling of accomplishment.

Children love to help make drop cookies, such as Gumdrop Rounds, where a delightful array of colors peek from the dough.

Youngsters under five can also have a part in cookie-making chores. Put them to work unwrapping caramels for Caramel Squares. Then let them assist with patting the crust in the pan.

Check on your children often when they are in the kitchen and offer assistance when appropriate. But, by all means, don't overreact when budding cooks and bakers make a mess. Teach them how to clean it up, and encourage them to perfect their baking skills.

No-Bake Chocolate-Cereal Squares

So easy, children can make them.

2 cups (12 oz.) semisweet chocolate pieces
3/4 cup crunchy or smooth peanut butter
1-1/2 cups granola

2 cups toasted-corn-cereal flakes
1/3 cup chopped unsalted dry-roasted peanuts

Grease an 8- or 9-inch-square baking pan. In top of a double boiler, combine chocolate pieces and peanut butter. Heat over hot but not boiling water until melted and smooth, stirring occasionally. Or, in a 2-quart glass bowl, melt together chocolate pieces and peanut butter in microwave oven on full power (HIGH) 2 to 2-1/2 minutes, stirring twice. With a fork, stir in granola and cereal until well coated. Spread evenly in greased baking pan. Top with peanuts, pressing in lightly. Refrigerate in pan. Cut chilled cookies into squares. Store in refrigerator. Makes about 25 (1-1/2-inch) cookies.

Granola Blondies

Butterscotch-flavor squares made chewy with granola.

1/4 cup vegetable oil
1 cup packed brown sugar
1 egg
1 teaspoon vanilla extract

3/4 cup all-purpose flour
1 teaspoon baking powder
1 cup granola with almonds

Preheat oven to 350F (175C). Grease an 8-inch-square baking pan. In a medium bowl, combine oil and brown sugar. Beat in egg and vanilla. Stir in flour, baking powder and granola until blended. Spread evenly in greased baking pan. Bake about 25 minutes. Do not overbake. While warm, cut into squares. Cool in pan. Makes 25 (1-1/2-inch) cookies.

Chewy Date-Nut Squares

Rich and chewy, these flourless squares go together in minutes.

2 eggs
1 teaspoon vanilla extract
3/4 cup packed brown sugar
2 teaspoons grated orange peel
1 teaspoon baking powder

3/4 cup fresh breadcrumbs
1 cup chopped pitted dates
1 cup chopped walnuts or pecans
Powdered sugar

Preheat oven to 325F (165C). Grease an 8- or 9-inch-square baking pan. In a medium bowl, combine eggs, vanilla, brown sugar, orange peel and baking powder. Stir in breadcrumbs, dates and nuts. Spread evenly in greased baking pan. Bake 35 to 45 minutes or until golden. Cool in pan. Sift powdered sugar over top. Cut cooled cookies into squares. Makes 25 (1-1/2-inch) cookies.

How to Make Rocky-Road Oaties

1/Press oat mixture evenly in greased, foil-lined pan.

2/Stir marshmallows into melted chocolate mixture.

Rocky-Road Oaties

If you like rocky road, you will love these candy-like cookies.

4 cups rolled oats
1 cup packed light-brown sugar
1/2 cup light corn syrup
6 tablespoons butter or margarine, melted

2 cups (12 oz.) semisweet chocolate pieces
1/2 cup crunchy peanut butter
2 cups miniature marshmallows

Preheat oven to 375F (190C). Line a 15" x 10" jelly-roll pan with foil; grease foil generously. In a large bowl, combine oats, brown sugar, corn syrup and melted butter or margarine, blending well. Press mixture evenly in greased, foil-lined pan. Bake 8 to 10 minutes or until light golden. Cool completely in pan. Meanwhile, in top of a double boiler, combine chocolate pieces and peanut butter. Heat over hot but not boiling water until melted, stirring occasionally. Remove pan from water. Stir in marshmallows. Immediately spread chocolate mixture evenly over cooled crust. Refrigerate. Cut chilled cookies into bars. Store in refrigerator, if desired. Makes 50 (2" x 1-1/2") cookies.

Flourless Peanut-Butter Cookies

Amazingly simple to prepare.

1 cup crunchy or smooth peanut butter
3/4 cup sugar
1 egg

1 teaspoon vanilla extract
Semisweet chocolate pieces, if desired

Preheat oven to 350F (175C). In a medium bowl, combine peanut butter, sugar, egg and vanilla until well blended. Shape dough into 1-inch balls. Place 2 inches apart on ungreased baking sheets. Flatten balls in crisscross pattern with tines of a fork or flatten slightly with bottom of a glass dipped in sugar. Press a chocolate piece in center of each cookie, if desired. Bake 8 to 10 minutes or until golden. Remove cookies from baking sheets; cool on racks. Makes about 48 (1-3/4-inch) cookies.

Chewy Graham-Cracker-Crumb Squares

An old favorite dating back to my childhood days.

1-1/2 cups graham-cracker crumbs
1 (14-oz.) can sweetened condensed milk
1 cup (6 oz.) semisweet chocolate pieces or
  peanut-butter-flavor pieces

1 cup chopped walnuts or almonds

Preheat oven to 350F (175C). Grease an 8- or 9-inch-square baking pan. In a medium bowl, stir together graham-cracker crumbs, sweetened condensed milk, chocolate or peanut-butter pieces and nuts. Spread evenly in greased baking pan. Bake 25 to 30 minutes or until golden. While hot, cut into squares. Cool in pan. Makes about 25 (1-1/2-inch) cookies.

Snappy Crackle Jiffy Squares

When the kids demand cookies right now, let them make these.

1/4 cup butter or margarine
1/2 cup crunchy peanut butter
3 cups miniature marshmallows

4 cups oven-toasted rice cereal
1/2 cup flaked or shredded coconut,
  if desired

Line an 8- or 9-inch-square baking pan with foil. In a large saucepan, combine butter or margarine and peanut butter. Heat over low heat until melted, stirring constantly. Add marshmallows; heat until melted, stirring constantly. Remove from heat. Stir in cereal and coconut, if desired, until completely coated with marshmallow mixture. Press mixture evenly in foil-lined baking pan. Let stand until set, about 1 hour. Cut cooled cookies into squares. Makes 25 (1-1/2-inch) cookies.

Tip *Store crisp cookies loosely covered; cover soft cookies with a tight-fitting lid.*

Cookie Pizza

Bake oatmeal-cookie dough with favorite toppings in a pizza pan; serve in wedges.

1/2 cup butter or margarine, room temperature
3/4 cup packed brown sugar
1 egg
1 teaspoon vanilla extract
3/4 cup all-purpose flour
Pinch of salt
1/2 teaspoon baking powder

1/2 teaspoon baking soda
1 cup rolled oats
1/2 cup flaked or shredded coconut
1 cup (6 oz.) semisweet chocolate pieces
1/2 cup chopped walnuts
1/2 cup yellow-tinted coconut, if desired
1/2 cup colored-candy-coated chocolate pieces, if desired

Preheat oven to 350F (175C). Grease a 12-inch pizza pan. In a medium bowl, beat together butter or margarine, brown sugar, egg and vanilla until light and fluffy. Add flour, salt, baking powder, baking soda and oats, beating until blended. Stir in plain coconut. Spread dough evenly in greased pizza pan. Sprinkle with chocolate pieces, walnuts and yellow coconut, if desired. Bake 13 to 15 minutes or until golden brown. Cool in pan. Garnish with candy pieces, if desired. Cut cooled cookie pizza into wedges. Makes about 12 cookie wedges.

Gumdrop Rounds

An array of colored gumdrops peek out of these cookies.

1 cup butter or margarine, room temperature
3/4 cup packed brown sugar
1 egg
1 teaspoon vanilla extract
1-1/2 cups all-purpose flour
1/2 teaspoon baking powder

1/2 teaspoon baking soda
1/4 teaspoon salt
1 cup rolled oats
3/4 cup chopped walnuts
1 cup cut-up colored gumdrops

Preheat oven to 350F (175C). In a large bowl, beat together butter or margarine, brown sugar, egg and vanilla until light and fluffy. Add flour, baking powder, baking soda and salt, beating until well blended. Stir in oats, walnuts and gumdrops. Drop by rounded teaspoonfuls, 1-1/2 inches apart, on ungreased baking sheets. Bake 12 to 14 minutes or until golden. Remove cookies from baking sheets; cool on racks. Makes 60 to 65 (1-3/4-inch) cookies.

Caramel Squares

Have the children help unwrap caramels to make these easy, sensational cookies.

Brown-Sugar Crust, page 96
1 (14-oz.) pkg. caramels, unwrapped
1/4 cup whipping cream

1 teaspoon vanilla extract
2 cups coarsely chopped pecans or toasted chopped almonds

Preheat oven to 350F (175C). Prepare Brown-Sugar Crust. Lightly grease a 13" x 9" baking pan. Pat dough evenly in bottom of greased baking pan. Bake 13 to 14 minutes or until light golden. Cool in pan. In a medium skillet, combine caramels and cream. Heat over low heat until melted and smooth, stirring occasionally. Remove from heat. Stir in vanilla and nuts. Carefully spread hot caramel mixture evenly over cooled crust. Cool in pan. Cut cooled cookies into squares. Makes 48 (1-1/2-inch) cookies.

Peanut-Butter-Candy Cookies

No baking required for these fabulous treats.

1/2 cup butter or margarine, melted
3/4 cup smooth or crunchy peanut butter
1 cup graham-cracker crumbs
1 cup powdered sugar

3/4 cup chopped peanuts, walnuts or raisins
1 cup (6 oz.) semisweet chocolate pieces, melted

Line an 8- or 9-inch-square baking pan with foil. In a medium bowl, combine melted butter or margarine and peanut butter until throughly blended. Add graham-cracker crumbs and powdered sugar, blending well. Stir in nuts or raisins. Press mixture evenly in foil-lined baking pan. Refrigerate in pan 1 hour. Spread evenly with melted chocolate. Refrigerate 15 minutes; then cut into squares. Store in refrigerator. Makes about 25 (1-1/2-inch) cookies.

Almost-Candy Cookies

My daughter likes this combination of peanut butter, chocolate and caramel.

1/2 recipe Peanut-Butter-Cookie Cutouts dough, page 116
1 cup (6 oz.) semisweet chocolate pieces

32 caramel candies, unwrapped
1/4 cup whipping cream
35 pecan halves

Preheat oven to 350F (175C). Press Peanut-Butter-Cookie Cutouts dough in bottom of an ungreased 11'' x 7'' baking pan. Bake 8 to 10 minutes or until light golden. Sprinkle with chocolate pieces; let stand 5 minutes or until melted. Spread evenly over crust. In a medium saucepan or skillet, combine caramels and whipping cream. Heat over low heat until melted and smooth, stirring frequently. Drizzle over top of melted chocolate; then with a knife spread evenly. Top with pecan halves, rounded-sides up, arranging in 7 rows of 5 each. Let stand until set. When set, cut into 35 pieces, with a pecan half in center of each. Makes about 35 (1-1/2-inch) cookies.

Orange-Fruit Balls

No cooking, no baking; ideal for young children to make.

3 cups vanilla-wafer crumbs
1/3 cup thawed frozen-orange-juice concentrate
3 tablespoons corn syrup

1/2 cup sunflower nuts
1 cup chopped dried fruit
Sifted powdered sugar

In a large bowl, combine vanilla-wafer crumbs, orange-juice concentrate and corn syrup, blending well. Stir in sunflower nuts and dried fruit. Shape into 1-inch balls. Roll in powdered sugar, coating completely. Store in refrigerator. Makes about 50 (1-inch) balls.

How to Make In-A-Hurry Gingerbread Cookies

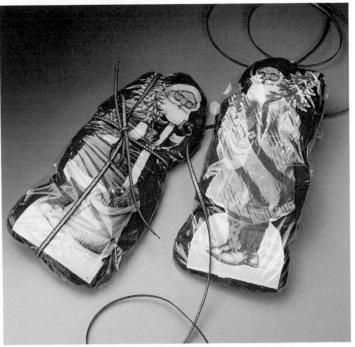

1/To use holiday-design stickers as cookie patterns, place sticker on unbaked dough. With a knife, cut around sticker as a pattern.

2/To prepare gingerbread as a gift, place sticker on top of cooled cookie. Wrap in plastic wrap and tie for an attractive gift.

In-A-Hurry Gingerbread Cookies

When time is short, let the kids use this dough for cutout cookies.

1 (14- or 14.5-oz.) pkg. gingerbread mix
4 to 5 tablespoons warm water
Raisins, if desired

Decorator Buttercream Icing, page 145,
  if desired

In a medium bowl, combine gingerbread mix and warm water until mixture clings together and forms a ball. It may be necessary to use your hands. Wrap and refrigerate until firm, at least 1 hour. To bake cookies, preheat oven to 350F (175C). Grease baking sheets. Between 2 sheets of waxed paper, roll dough 1/4 inch thick. With lightly floured cookie cutters, cut into desired shapes. Place 1 inch apart on greased baking sheets. If you don't plan to frost the cookies, add raisins for faces and buttons on gingerbread people and Santas, if desired. Bake 9 to 11 minutes or until set. Cool 2 to 3 minutes on baking sheets; then remove to racks to cool completely. Prepare Decorator Buttercream Icing, if desired. Frost and decorate as desired. Makes 10 to 12 large (6-1/2" x 2 1/2") cookies.

Tip

For a holiday decoration, tie gingerbread cookies to a rattan wreath or Christmas tree. Let each guest take one home.

Specialty Cookies

These are fun cookies. You'll want to consider baking them when you have time and energy to get involved in a cookie-making project. Involve the children, the entire family or even friends, as time and patience allow. Many of these suggestions are complicated, but results are well worth the effort.

What child wouldn't have visions of sugarplums dancing in his head when he spots the enchanting Fairy-Tale Gingerbread House? This masterpiece is entirely edible. Feature it as the center attraction of your holiday decorations.

Don't be intimidated by the construction details of a gingerbread house. Like anything else, it is a matter of getting organized. Allow time to accomplish it.

If a from-scratch gingerbread-house creation is more than you want to make, opt for a less-elaborate model built with graham crackers. Easy enough for youngsters to make and decorate, it's a super-fun project.

Have-A-Heart-Valentine Cookies are a novel and delicious way to send greetings to family, teachers or friends. A foil-covered piece of cardboard or a festive basket lined with a doily are good for packaging.

When you're in the mood for another rewarding afternoon of baking, recruit the children to help bake a batch of edible cookie puzzles. If puzzles aren't appealing, use crisp lemony shortbread dough for edible greeting cards.

Meringue Mushrooms are designed for impressing your most discriminating guests. Pile them in a basket as a table decoration at your next party. Pass them for dessert and sit back and enjoy the raves. Prepare in advance and store loosely covered at room temperature. They'll last for weeks.

When it comes to creating cutout cookies, choose the versatile Gingerbread Cookie recipe. It is one recipe you can get going on immediately as no chilling is required. If you want to hang cookies on a Christmas tree or door knob, cut out ribbon-threading holes near the top of the unbaked cookies with a plastic straw. Adorn baked cookies with frosting paints, colored candies or miniature baked and frosted cookie-dough shapes—or whatever strikes your fancy.

Black-Eyed Susans

Flower cookies stand in little flower pots for decorations and gifts.

1/2 cup butter or margarine, room temperature	1/2 teaspoon baking powder
	Pinch of salt
1/2 cup smooth peanut butter	Raisin-Orange Filling, see below
3/4 cup sugar	Vanilla-Buttercream Icing, page 153,
1 egg	if desired
1 teaspoon vanilla extract	Few drops yellow food coloring, if desired
1-1/4 cups all-purpose flour	

Raisin-Orange Filling:

1 cup chopped raisins	3 tablespoons sugar
1/2 cup orange juice	Pinch of salt
3/4 teaspoon grated orange peel	

In a medium bowl, beat together butter or margarine, peanut butter, sugar, egg and vanilla until light and fluffy. Add flour, baking powder and salt, beating until well blended. Wrap and refrigerate dough 1 hour. Meanwhile, prepare Raisin-Orange Filling; set aside to cool. To bake cookies, preheat oven to 350F (175C). On a floured surface, roll dough 3/16 inch thick. Using a floured, round 2-3/4-inch cookie cutter with a scalloped edge, cut into rounds. Place half the rounds, 1-1/2 inches apart, on an ungreased baking sheet. Place a heaping teaspoonful of Raisin-Orange Filling on each round, spreading to within 1/2 inch of edge. Cut 3/4-inch holes from centers of remaining dough rounds. Place on top of raisin-topped dough rounds, pressing edges together lightly. Bake 10 to 12 minutes or until light golden. Cool 5 minutes on pan; then remove to racks to cool completely. If desired, prepare Vanilla-Buttercream Icing and tint yellow. Pipe icing around edges of cooled cookies to simulate flowers. Makes about 16 (3-inch) filled cookies.

Raisin-Orange Filling:
In a small saucepan, combine raisins, orange juice, orange peel, sugar and salt. Bring to a boil over high heat, stirring occasionally. Reduce heat to medium; simmer 15 minutes or until thickened, stirring frequently.

Variation

Flower Pops: To bake cookies on wooden ice-cream sticks, lay ice-cream stick onto each bottom dough round so that about 1-1/2-inches of the stick is on the dough and the rest of the stick serves as the stem. Press stick lightly in place. Top with raisin filling and top dough round as above, pressing 2 dough circles firmly together around edge. Bake as directed. Cool cookies completely on baking sheet before removing. Decorate as directed. Stand cookie flowers in floral clay or styrofoam in small clay flower pots. For added decoration, spray-paint pots in desired colors before adding cookie flowers. Decorate around top edge of flower pot with a colorful band of braid for a special centerpiece or gift.

Tip *If you don't have a pastry bag, make one by placing icing in a clean paper envelope. Cut off one corner. Carefully press icing through opening.*

Pizzelles

You'll need a pizzelle or krumkake iron to make these Italian cookies.

6 eggs
1-1/2 cups sugar
1 cup butter or margarine, melted, cooled
2 tablespoons anise extract or
   vanilla extract

3-1/4 to 3-1/2 cups all-purpose flour
4 teaspoons baking powder

If using an electric pizzelle iron containing round 5-inch grids, preheat according to manufacturer's directions. In a large bowl, beat eggs. Gradually add sugar; continue to beat until smooth. Beat in butter or margarine and anise extract or vanilla. Beat in flour and baking powder until thoroughly blended. Batter will be sticky enough to be dropped by spoon. Drop a generous tablespoonful of batter in center of each heated grid. Immediately close iron, squeezing handles together. Scrape off any batter that flows out around edges. Bake in electric iron 30 seconds or until light golden brown. If using hand-held iron, follow manufacturer's directions for baking. When golden, loosen Pizzelle with fork or point of knife and carefully remove to a rack to cool. Store Pizzelles in a tightly covered container. Use within 2 to 3 weeks. Makes 48 to 50 (5-inch) Pizzelles.

Variations

Chocolate Pizzelles: Omit anise extract, using vanilla instead. Melt 3 ounces unsweetened chocolate with butter; add as directed. Increase sugar to 2 cups and baking powder to 4-1/2 teaspoons. Proceed as directed above.

Cocoa Pizzelles: Add 1/2 cup unsweetened cocoa along with flour. Increase sugar to 2 cups and baking powder to 4-1/2 teaspoons. Proceed as directed above.

Scandinavian Rosettes

Popular throughout Scandinavia, these crisp fried cookies are Swedish in origin.

Oil for deep-frying
1 egg
1 teaspoon granulated sugar
Pinch of salt
1/2 cup milk

1/2 cup all-purpose flour
1-1/2 to 2 teaspoons ground cinnamon or
   1 tablespoon orange or lemon extract
Powdered sugar

In a medium saucepan, pour oil to a 3-inch depth. Heat oil to 375F (190C) or until a 1-inch cube of bread turns brown in 50 seconds. Meanwhile, in a medium bowl, whisk together egg, granulated sugar and salt. Whisk in milk, flour and cinnamon or orange or lemon extract until thoroughly blended and batter is smooth. For each rosette, preheat rosette iron in hot oil 1 minute, allowing excess oil to drip off. Dip hot iron in batter until it comes 3/4 of the way up the iron. Do not let batter go over top of iron. If iron isn't hot enough, batter will not stick. Plunge batter-coated iron into hot oil, frying until active bubbling stops and rosettes are golden, 30 to 45 seconds. Be careful not to overbrown. Remove from oil; carefully loosen rosette with fork. Drain on paper towels. Cool. Before serving, sift powdered sugar over tops. Makes 18 to 20 (3-inch) rosettes.

 **Tip**

Be sure to dip rosette iron in hot oil before dipping into batter.

How to Make Pizzelles

1/Drop a generous tablespoonful of batter in center of each heated grid. Immediately close iron.

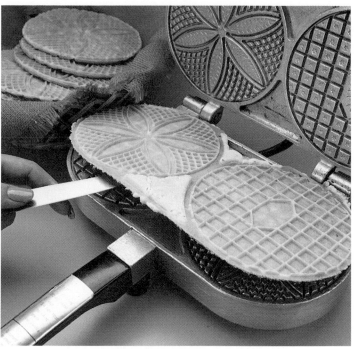

2/When golden, loosen pizzelle with a fork or knife point and carefully remove to a rack to cool.

Krumkake

Use a krumkake iron, available at cookware shops, to make these Scandinavian specialties.

3 eggs
1/2 cup granulated sugar
5 tablespoons butter or margarine, melted
3 tablespoons whipping cream

1-1/2 teaspoons vanilla extract
3/4 cup all-purpose flour
Mocha-Cream Filling, see below

Mocha-Cream Filling:
2 cups whipping cream
1/4 cup powdered sugar

2 tablespoons unsweetened cocoa
1 tablespoon instant-coffee powder

Grease a krumkake iron with shortening. Heat iron over medium heat of electric or gas range. In a medium bowl, whisk together eggs, granulated sugar, melted butter or margarine, cream and vanilla until thoroughly blended. Add flour, whisking until smooth. For each cookie, spoon a scant tablespoon of batter in center of greased round 5-inch iron. Close, squeezing handles together gently. Scrape off any batter that flows out around edges. Bake 20 to 25 seconds on each side or until light golden. Keep iron over heat at all times. Loosen and remove cookie with a knife. Leave cookie flat or immediately roll hot cookie around a wooden cone or roll into a cylinder. Cool, seam-side down, on racks. Serve plain or fill with Mocha-Cream Filling immediately before serving. Makes about 30 (5-inch) krumkakes.

Mocha-Cream Filling:
In a large bowl, beat whipping cream with electric mixer at high speed until soft peaks form. Beat in powdered sugar, cocoa and instant-coffee powder until well blended and cream holds its shape.

Cookie Circus Cage

Plan plenty of time for this creative cookie project.

1 cup vegetable shortening	1 teaspoon ground allspice
1 cup packed brown sugar	1-1/2 teaspoons ground ginger
3 eggs	1/4 teaspoon salt
2 cups light molasses	2 tablespoons grated orange peel
8 cups all-purpose flour	1 recipe Gingerbread House &
2 teaspoons baking soda	Cookie Icing, page 147
2-1/2 tablespoons ground cinnamon	Brown paste food coloring

In a large bowl, beat together shortening, brown sugar, eggs and molasses until blended. Beat in flour, baking soda, cinnamon, allspice, ginger, salt and orange peel until blended. Divide dough into 2 equal portions. Wrap each portion and refrigerate several hours or overnight. To bake, pre-heat oven to 300F (150C). Line 2 (18" x 12") sheet-cake pans with heavy-duty foil; grease foil. On a lightly floured sheet of waxed paper, roll each portion of dough to fit lined pans. Invert dough onto greased, lined pans; peel off paper. Using your fingers, smooth dough into corners. Place pattern pieces on dough as per the diagram, page 156. Cut around pieces, but do not remove dough from pan. Cut windows in cage, but do not remove dough. Bake dough, 1 pan at a time, in center of oven about 70 minutes. Avoid overbrowning. The long baking time is necessary for a sturdy and thoroughly baked cookie. Remove from oven; immediately re-cut pieces, removing excess baked dough. Save excess rectangles from cage sides to cut and use as stands for circus animals, if desired. Allow large pieces to cool in pan, loosening carefully underneath with a spatula while still warm. Cool pieces overnight.

To Assemble Cookie Circus Cage: Cover a 12-1/2" x 7" cardboard rectangle with foil. Prepare Gingerbread-House & Cookie Icing. Keep icing covered with a damp towel during assembly to prevent drying. Color 3/4 icing brown. Place brown icing in a large pastry bag fitted with a round 1/4- to 1/2-inch diameter decorating tube until 2/3 full. Place base of cookie cage on cardboard piece, securing underneath in a few places with brown icing. Pipe brown icing along sides of base and on top of ends of base. Stand end pieces of cage upright in place on top of bottom cage cookie, pressing against frosting at base. Pipe a strip of icing up edges of end pieces where one side of cage will be attached. Stand side of cage upright in place, pressing lightly to join. Hold the pieces upright in place for a few minutes until icing has set. Repeat with remaining cage side-wall. Wipe off any excess frosting before it becomes dry. Let stand 1 hour or more until firmly set. Cover an additional 11-3/4" x 5-1/2" cardboard rectangle with foil. Pipe a little brown icing 1 inch in from each of the 4 corners. Place top cage cookie piece on foil-covered cardboard, pressing down gently to secure; set aside. Cardboard acts as extra support for the cage top. Stand decorated lion or other circus animal, pages 144, 8 and 9, inside circus cage. Pipe a brown-icing strip on top of ends of cage. Also pipe small rounds of icing inside along sides of cage at about the same level where top of cage will join sides. Set top of cage in, resting on ends and pressing gently in place. Press sides gently into top to secure. Decorate wheels and attach to each side of cage with brown icing. Decorate cage as desired. Let cage dry overnight. Makes 1 circus cage.

Tip *You may wish to leave your circus cage open at the top. If so, don't cut a top piece for the cage.*

Circus Animals & Party Carousels *Photo on page 142.*

Perfect as individual party favors—kids will love them.

2 recipes Gingerbread Cookies, page 149	**Plastic drinking straws**
2 recipes Frosting Paint & Icing, page 149	**Carousel tops**
Assorted paste food colors	
1/2 recipe Gingerbread House & Cookie Icing, page 147	

Prepare Gingerbread Cookie dough. Preheat oven to 350F (175C). Grease baking sheets. Roll dough on a floured surface to 1/4 inch thickness. Using floured cutters or patterns given on pages 8 and 9 , cut out circus animals such as a lion, bear, elephant or giraffe and a clown. Also cut 6 to 8 rocking horses from rolled dough. Roll a portion of dough 1/2 inch thick. Cut 6 to 8 (2-5/8-inch-diameter) rounds for carousel bases. Make a depression or groove across the center of each cookie base using a wooden-spoon handle. Place cookies, 1-inch apart, on greased baking sheets. Place carousel bases on a separate baking sheet. Bake 9 to 13 minutes or until firm but not dark. Baking time will depend on size and thickness of dough. Cool on baking sheets; then remove to racks. Let stand overnight to dry thoroughly.

To frost Circus Animals and horses for Party Carousels: Prepare 1 recipe Frosting Paint & Icing. Divide frosting among 7 small bowls. Tint each portion a different color. Suggested colors include white, brown, black, gray, yellow, gold and orange. After blending in food color, thin each with a few drops of water until mixture reaches consistency of thick paint. Using an artist's brush, paint entire cookie surface desired color. Dry completely on a flat surface overnight. Prepare a second recipe of Frosting Paint & Icing. Divide frosting among 8 small bowls. Tint each portion a different color. **Do not thin with water.** Suggested colors include brown, black, yellow, gold, orange, green, blue and red. While decorating cookies, keep frosting covered to keep from drying out. Spoon frosting into separate pastry bags fitted with desired decorating tubes. Pipe decorations such as faces or designs. Make designs as simple or elaborate as time allows. Allow cookies to dry completely on a flat surface. Cut excess reserved baked dough pieces from circus cage, as necessary, to make stands to attach to back of circus animals. Attach pieces at an angle to back of circus animals with plenty of brown frosting. Prop up and allow to dry thoroughly. Cardboard pieces may also be used for stands, attaching with frosting in the same manner.

To Assemble Party Carousels: Prepare Gingerbread House & Cookie Icing, tinting as desired. Spread icing on round bases of carousels. Stand a decorated horse in the icing-filled groove on each base. Hold until set firmly. Attach a plastic drinking straw to back of each horse, using white icing. Each straw should be propped in frosting in carousel base and should extend about 2-1/4 inches above horse's head. Let carousels stand to dry completely, checking often to make sure they dry upright. When dry, pipe an icing design around carousel base with a small decorating tube. Let stand until dry. When dry, attach a paper carousel to the top of each straw or insert a plastic carousel top, available at cake-decorating-supply stores, into top of straw. Place animals and clown around circus cage as desired. Use carousels as individual party favors.

Meringue Mushrooms

Mushroom-shape cookies arranged in a basket make festive edible party-table decorations.

3 egg whites
Pinch of salt
1/8 teaspoon cream of tartar
3/4 cup sugar

1/2 teaspoon vanilla extract
1/4 to 1/3 cup chocolate-coating wafers,
  melted
Unsweetened cocoa

Preheat oven to 200F (95C). Line 2 baking sheets with foil. To hold foil in place, place a little vegetable oil under foil in each corner of baking sheet. In a large bowl, beat egg whites, salt and cream of tartar with electric mixer at high speed until soft peaks form. Gradually add sugar, 1 tablespoon at a time, beating at high speed until stiff and glossy, about 5 minutes. Beat in vanilla. Spoon meringue into a large pastry bag fitted with a large round 1/2-inch-diameter decorating tube, filling half-full at a time. To pipe mushroom stems, hold filled bag at right angle to baking sheet with point of tube almost touching foil. Squeeze bag gently while slowly lifting it straight up to form stems 1 to 1-1/4 inches high, ending with a point. Base of stems should be wider than top for support. Pipe stems 1/2 to 1 inch apart. To pipe caps, place tip of filled bag at right angle close to foil and squeeze out meringue to form a small mound about 1-1/4 to 1-1/2 inches in diameter and 3/4 inch high. Pipe 1/2 to 1 inch apart. With tip of knife, smooth tops of stems and caps, removing any points. Bake both baking sheets at the same time in 1 oven 1-1/4 hours or until meringues are crisp and dry and can be easily peeled from foil. They should not brown. Turn off oven and let meringues cool in oven. Peel cool meringues from foil. Carefully cut off a tiny portion of tops of stems, making them parallel with bases. To assemble mushrooms, using a small spatula or knife, spread a thin layer of melted chocolate over underneath side of mushroom cap, piling up a little chocolate in the center. Place top of mushroom stem (side you have cut) in center of chocolate on mushroom cap; hold a few seconds. Then carefully stand up mushroom on foil or waxed paper on a flat surface. Rearrange cap and stem, if necessary, to steady mushroom so it doesn't topple. Let stand until set. Mushrooms set up very quickly when candy-coating chocolate is used. When chocolate has set, sift a very small amount of cocoa over mushrooms. Store covered, but not airtight. Makes about 25 (1-3/4" x 1-1/2") mushrooms.

Decorator Buttercream Icing

This works well for both decorating and frosting cookies.

1 (1-lb.) pkg. powdered sugar (3-3/4 cups)
1/4 cup butter or margarine,
  room temperature
1/4 cup vegetable shortening
3 to 4 tablespoons water, milk or
  strained fruit juice

1 teaspoon vanilla extract or
  other flavoring, as desired
1 tablespoon light corn syrup
Paste food colors, as desired

In a medium bowl, beat together powdered sugar, butter or margarine, shortening, water, milk or fruit juice, vanilla or other flavoring and corn syrup using electric mixer at high speed 7 to 8 minutes. Tint icing, if desired. Use to frost and decorate cookies. Pipe through a large pastry bag fitted with desired decorating tube. Or, spread on cookies with a knife and decorate with sprinkles or colored sugar. Keep icing covered when not in use. Store in refrigerator. Makes about 2 cups icing.

Variation

Chocolate Decorator Buttercream Icing: Use milk, increasing to 6 tablespoons. Add 6 tablespoons unsweetened cocoa before starting to beat mixture.

Fairy-Tale Gingerbread House

Photo on pages 154 and 155

Perfect as a centerpiece at a child's party or for a holiday decoration.

1 cup vegetable shortening
1 cup packed brown sugar
1 cup molasses
2 eggs
2-1/2 teaspoons ground cinnamon
2 teaspoons ground ginger
1 teaspoon ground allspice

1/2 teaspoon ground cloves
1/4 teaspoon salt
6 cups all-purpose flour
2 tablespoons baking powder
2 recipes Gingerbread-House & Cookie Icing, opposite
Assorted candies

In a large bowl, beat together shortening, brown sugar, molasses and eggs until thoroughly blended. Beat in cinnamon, ginger, allspice, cloves and salt. Add flour and baking powder, beating until well blended. Dough will be sticky. Divide dough into 2 equal portions. Wrap each portion in a plastic bag. Refrigerate 1 hour or longer. To bake gingerbread, preheat oven to 300F (150C). Line 2 (18'' x 12'') sheet-cake pans with heavy-duty foil; grease foil. Or, use 1 pan and reuse after baking. Using a rolling pin, roll each portion of dough out on 1 greased foil-lined pan in an even layer, filling pan completely. Place 2 side and 2 roof patterns on 1 pan. Place front and back house patterns on other pan. Cut around them carefully; do not separate and remove dough from pan. Cut scraps along 1 side with small cookie cutters, making snowmen, trees or angels, but do not remove from pan. These cookies will be used to decorate the yard around the house. Bake pans of dough, 1 at a time, in center of oven 55 to 65 minutes. Watch carefully to avoid overbrowning. Long baking time is necessary for a hard cookie—important to make a sturdy house. Remove pan from oven; immediately re-cut dough pieces, removing any excess gingerbread. Remove small dough pieces, including cookies, to racks to cool. Let large house pieces cool in pan, loosening carefully underneath them with a spatula while still warm. Allow house pieces to dry overnight. Assembly instructions on page 148.

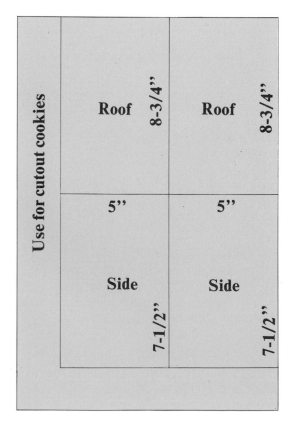

Gingerbread House

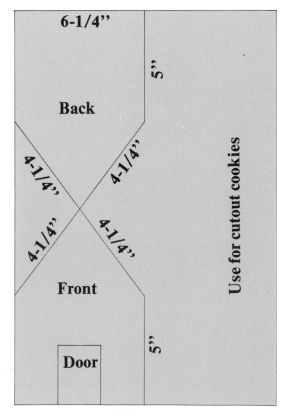

How to Make Fairy-Tale Gingerbread House

1/Using a rolling pin, roll out dough on foil-lined pan in an even layer, filling pan completely.

2/Place pattern pieces on dough according to drawing. Cut around pieces, but do not remove dough from pan. Cut scraps along side with cookie cutters.

Gingerbread-House & Cookie Icing

Use as cement when building cookie houses or to frost and decorate cookies.

4 egg whites
1 (1-lb.) pkg. powdered sugar (3-3/4 cups)

1/4 teaspoon cream of tartar

In a medium bowl, beat together egg whites, powdered sugar and cream of tartar with electric mixer at low speed until blended. Turn mixer to high speed; continue beating 7 to 10 minutes until thick and soft peaks form and a knife drawn through mixture leaves a clean-cut path. Use immediately or cover and store in airtight container in refrigerator. Use within 1 to 2 days. Once you begin working with the icing, keep it covered with a damp towel to prevent drying out. This icing dries hard. Makes about 3-3/4 cups icing.

Variation

Tint icing with paste colors or food coloring, as desired. Paste colors, available at cake-decorating-supply stores, are much stronger and give deeper colors.

To Assemble House: Prepare Gingerbread-House & Cookie Icing. Keep icing covered with a damp towel during assembly or it will dry out. Place icing in a large pastry bag fitted with a large plain round 1/4- to 1/2-inch-diameter decorating tube, filling half-full at a time. Use a round 16- to 18-inch-diameter styrofoam or cardboard piece for base. Draw lines at a right angle on the base where you want the front and left-side wall of house to stand. Ice over the lines using bag filled with icing. Place side wall upright in place; then pipe a strip of icing up edge where front wall will attach to it. Stand front wall in place attaching to side wall at a right angle. Hold the pieces upright for a few minutes until icing has set. Then prop walls up placing a heavy jar in corner for support. Let stand 30 minutes or longer until icing sets. Remove jar. With icing, cement right-side wall of house to front, piping icing strip on base and on edge of front wall as before. Put icing on base and on side walls where back will attach. Stand back in place. Let stand about 30 minutes or until set. Ice top edges of house; lay roof pieces over them, using jar or can under roof overhangs to prevent slippage while drying. Roof pieces should meet but not overlap. Fill any space between them with icing. Check house and make sure all seams are filled with icing. Let house stand until all icing has dried completely. Frost roof with icing and decorate with assorted candies, as desired. Using a large pastry bag fitted with a small round decorating tube, decorate sides, front and back of house with windows, shutters and flowers. Icing can be tinted, as desired. Add candy pieces. Decorate door. Decorate base of house or yard by spreading completely with white icing. Use candies to make walkway leading up to house. Arrange striped candies around edge of yard for fence. Decorate house and yard as elaborately or simply as desired and time allows. Attach front door to house by applying a strip of icing to door opening and base and standing door in place. Decorate assorted shaped cookies such as miniature gingerbreadmen, snowmen or others. Stand decorated cookies in yard using icing as cement. Makes 1 (9" x 9") gingerbread house. For a photo of completed house, refer to pages 154 and 155.

Photo on pages 154 and 155 clockwise: Fairy-Tale Gingerbread House, pages 146–148; Santa's Whiskers, page 50; Melting Moments, page 73; Buttery Nut Rossettes, page 95; Cookie Candy Canes, page 75; Melting Moments, page 73; Mrs. Arnold's Spritz Cookies, pages 66–67; and Cheese Wafers, page 54. Center: Fruitcake Drops, page 39.

How to Make Fairy-Tale Gingerbread House

3/Join front, sides and back as directed in recipe. Ice top edges of house; lay roof pieces over them. Roof pieces should meet but not overlap.

4/Decorate house as desired using a variety of colored-candy pieces and icing. Complete yard with white icing for snow and decorated cutout cookies.

Gingerbread Cookies

Prepare and bake immediately—no refrigeration is necessary.

1/2 cup butter or margarine,	**1 teaspoon baking soda**
room temperature	**2 teaspoons ground cinnamon**
1/2 cup packed brown sugar	**1 teaspoon ground ginger**
1/2 cup molasses	**1/2 teaspoon ground nutmeg**
1 egg	**1/2 teaspoon ground allspice**
3 cups all-purpose flour	**Frosting Paint & Icing, below**

Preheat oven to 350F (175C). Grease baking sheets. In a large bowl, beat together butter or margarine, brown sugar, molasses and egg until fluffy. Add flour, baking soda, cinnamon, ginger, nutmeg and allspice, beating until blended. Use immediately or wrap and refrigerate up to 1 week. On a floured surface, roll dough 1/4 inch thick. With lightly floured cookie cutters, cut into desired shapes. Place 1 inch apart on greased baking sheets. If cookies are to be used as Christmas-tree ornaments, use a plastic drinking straw to cut a hole in each cookie, 1/2 inch from top edge, removing excess dough. Bake 8 to 12 minutes, depending on cookie size, or until firm but not dark. Cool 10 minutes on pan; then remove to racks to cool. Prepare Frosting Paint & Icing, tinting colors and thinning with water as desired. Decorate cookies, as desired, using artist's brushes to paint on thinned icing mixture and using a pastry bag fitted with desired decorating tube to pipe thicker icing. Allow icing to dry between applications of additional layers of color or design. Let stand until set. Makes about 20 (5-inch) cookies.

Variation

Giant Gingerbread Cookies: Divide dough into 2 equal portions. On a greased and lightly floured baking sheet, roll each portion into a 14" x 11" rectangle. Using desired paper patterns about 10" x 7", cut out 2 giant cookies from each dough portion. Arrange 2 cookies, 1-1/2 inches apart, on each greased baking sheet. Re-roll remaining dough scraps; cut out another giant cookie or smaller cookies. Bake 12 to 14 minutes or until firm, watching carefully to avoid overbaking. Cool on baking sheets; then remove to flat surface, such as cardboard, to store. Decorate with Frosting Paint & Icing. Makes about 5 large (10" x 7") cookies.

Frosting Paint & Icing

Versatile frosting which can also be thinned and used as paint.

3 egg whites	**Paste food colors**
1 (1-lb.) pkg. powdered sugar (3-3/4 cups)	**Water**
1/2 teaspoon cream of tartar	

In a large bowl, combine egg whites, powdered sugar and cream of tartar. Beat with an electric mixer at low speed until blended. Increase speed to high and beat until mixture is thick and stiff and a knife drawn through mixture leaves a clean-cut path, 7 to 10 minutes. Spread on cookies with a knife or pipe on cookies using a pastry bag fitted with desired decorating tube. To use as paint, divide frosting among small bowls. Tint each portion as desired, and thin with a few drops of water until mixture reaches consistency of thick paint. Using artist brushes, paint cookies, allowing each color to dry before adding another color or details. When cookies are completely iced and dry, wrap individually in plastic wrap and tie with colored yarn. Cut any plastic wrap extending above yarn down to about 1 inch to make a neater cookie package. Makes about 2-3/4 cups icing.

Have-A-Big-Heart Valentines

A great gift for your sweetheart, teacher, boss, parent or grandparent.

1 cup butter or margarine, room temperature
1-1/3 cups packed brown sugar
2 eggs
2 teaspoons vanilla extract
2 teaspoons grated orange peel, if desired
2-1/4 cups all-purpose flour
1 teaspoon baking soda
1/4 teaspoon salt
2 cups (12 oz.) semisweet chocolate pieces,
   butterscotch-flavor pieces or
   peanut-butter-flavor pieces
2 cups chopped walnuts
Vanilla-Buttercream Icing, page 153,
   if desired

Preheat oven to 375F (190C). Grease 3 (9-inch) heart-shape cake pans. Line bottoms with waxed paper, cut to fit; grease paper. In a large bowl, beat together butter or margarine, brown sugar, eggs, vanilla and orange peel, if desired, until light and fluffy. Add flour, baking soda and salt, beating until blended. Stir in chocolate, butterscotch or peanut-butter pieces and walnuts. Divide dough into 3 equal portions. Spread each portion in a greased waxed-paper-lined cake pan. Bake 15 minutes or until light golden brown. Cool 5 minutes in pans; then loosen edges with knife and carefully turn out onto racks to cool completely. While warm, remove waxed paper from bottoms. Decorate or write messages or names on cooled cookies with Vanilla-Buttercream Icing, if desired. Makes 3 (9-inch) cookie hearts.

Variation

Giant Cookie Rounds: Grease and line 3 round 8- or 9-inch cake pans with waxed paper; grease again. Proceed as directed above.

Graham-Cracker Houses

A great holiday project for children.

Gingerbread-House & Cookie Icing, page 147
18 graham crackers (double squares
   measuring 5" x 2-1/2")
Assorted trimmings such as raisins, nuts,
   chocolate pieces, pretzels, cereal,
   marshmallows and candies

Prepare Gingerbread-House & Cookie Icing. Cover 3 (9-inch) round or square pieces of cardboard with foil. Each will be the base of 1 house. For each house, stand 4 graham crackers on edge in a square on foil-covered cardboard, applying Gingerbread-House & Cookie Icing with a knife to bottom and side edges of house front, back and walls, fitting crackers together and holding them in place as you work so icing will set. When house is fairly sturdy, apply icing to top edges and place 2 crackers together at an angle for the roof. Seal roof peak with icing. Frost and decorate with assorted trimmings as desired, using icing as cement to hold trimmings in place. Decorated houses make good table centerpieces and will keep several weeks in a dry place. Makes 3 small houses.

Tip

For support, build houses around 2 clean empty 1/2-pint milk cartons placed side-by-side on their sides.

How to Make Lemony Cookie Puzzles

1/Cut each dough rectangle into 4 equal pieces. Each piece will be 1 puzzle. Using a sharp knife or cookie cutters, cut each puzzle into 5 or 6 pieces.

2/Decorate and frost cooled puzzles with icing and assorted candies, as desired. Wrap and present as a gift.

Lemony Cookie Puzzles

Let children cut each puzzle into five or six pieces freehand or using cutters.

1 cup butter or margarine, room temperature
3/4 cup granulated sugar
3/4 cup powdered sugar
1 egg
1 teaspoon lemon extract

1-1/2 tablespoons grated lemon peel
2-3/4 to 3 cups all-purpose flour
2 recipes Vanilla-Buttercream Icing,
  opposite, colored as desired

In a large bowl, beat together butter or margarine, granulated sugar, powdered sugar, egg, lemon extract and lemon peel until light and fluffy. Add flour, beating until blended. Divide dough into 2 equal portions. Wrap and refrigerate 1 hour or longer. To bake cookies, preheat oven to 300F (150C). Line 2 baking sheets with foil. Roll each dough portion into a 13" x 10" rectangle on a foil-lined baking sheet, flouring top as necessary and making sure edges are even. Cut each dough rectangle into 4 equal pieces, each measuring 6-1/2" x 5" but do not separate. Each of these pieces will form 1 puzzle. With a sharp knife or cookie cutters, cut each puzzle into 5 or 6 pieces, but do not separate pieces. Abstract free-form designs are good. Bake 15 to 20 minutes or until set. Cookies should be pale in color. Do not let them brown. Immediately re-cut puzzle pieces as marked. While warm, carefully trim and even edges of cookies, if necessary. Cool on pans. Prepare Vanilla-Buttercream Icing. Decorate and frost cooled puzzles as desired with icing. Icing looks especially attractive piped around edges of each puzzle piece, using a pastry bag fitted with a star decorating tube. Store airtight at room temperature up to 1 week. Freeze for longer storage. Makes 8 (6-1/2" x 5") cookie puzzles.

Vanilla-Buttercream Icing

A versatile icing. Vary the flavor and tint colors, as desired, to complement the cookies.

**1/4 cup butter or margarine,
   room temperature**
1 cup powdered sugar
Pinch of salt

1 teaspoon vanilla extract
1/2 to 1 teaspoon orange extract
1 tablespoon whipping cream or milk
Paste food colors, if desired

In a small bowl, beat together butter or margarine, sugar, salt, vanilla, orange extract and cream or milk until fluffy. Tint with food colors, if desired. Use to decorate cookies, either spreading on or piping on. Makes about 1 cup icing.

Variation

Chocolate-Buttercream Icing: Add 2 ounces melted unsweetened chocolate to icing.

Baklava Supreme

A not-too-sweet version of the popular Middle-Eastern dessert.

Sugar Syrup, see below
**1-1/2 cups unsalted butter, melted,
   clarified**
**4 cups finely chopped walnuts
   (about 1 lb.)**

4 teaspoons ground cinnamon
1/3 cup sugar
**1 (1-lb.) pkg. filo pastry sheets (sheets
   should each measure about 17" x 12")**

Sugar Syrup:
1-1/4 cups sugar
3/4 cup water

3 whole cloves
1 tablespoon lemon juice

Prepare Sugar Syrup. Preheat oven to 350F (175C). Brush an 18" x 12" sheet-cake pan with clarified butter. In a medium bowl, combine walnuts, cinnamon and sugar. Open and stack filo sheets on a damp towel. Cover with plastic wrap or a damp towel to prevent drying out. Layer half the filo sheets (about 12 to 15) in baking pan, brushing each sheet with clarified butter. Spread half of nut mixture over layered filo sheets. Butter next filo sheet on both sides; then place on top of nuts. Add 6 more filo sheets, brushing each with butter. Spread with remaining nut mixture. Butter next filo sheet on both sides and place on top of nuts. Top with remaining filo sheets, brushing each with butter. With a sharp knife, cut pastry into diamond-shape pieces. Do not remove pastry from pan. Brush top with remaining butter. Bake 50 to 60 minutes or until golden. Pour Sugar Syrup over hot pastry. Let stand several hours or overnight before serving. May be kept covered 1 week at room temperature. Freeze for longer storage. Makes about 50 (3" x 1-1/2") pieces.

Sugar Syrup:

In a medium saucepan, combine sugar, water and cloves. Bring to a boil, stirring often. Reduce heat and simmer 10 minutes. Stir in lemon juice. Set aside to cool. Before using, remove cloves.

Tip

To clarify butter, melt butter over low heat in a skillet. Let stand a few minutes. Skim off and discard white whey or milk solids that rise to the top. Also, do not use any milky residue that may sink to the bottom of the skillet. The clear yellow liquid is clarified butter.

Cookie Circus Cage

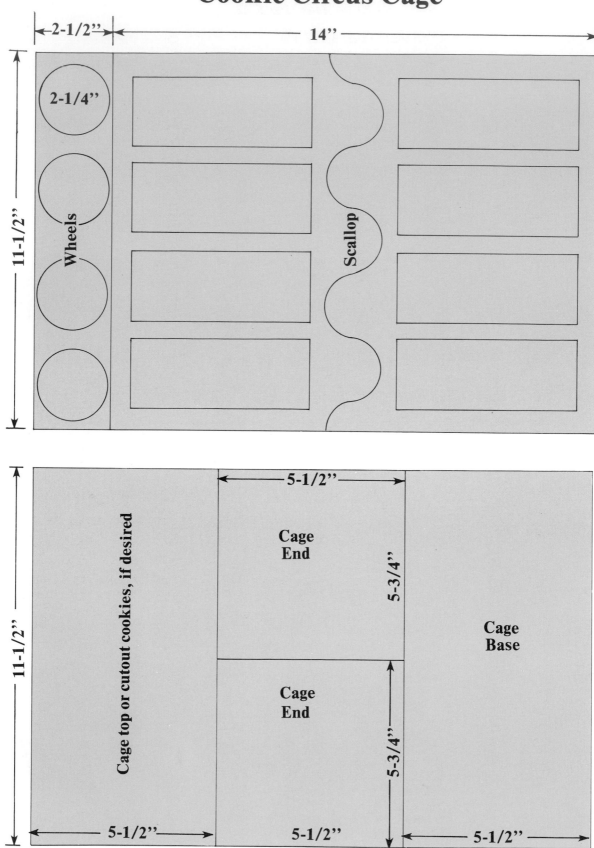

2-1/2"

14"

2-1/4"

Wheels

Scallop

11-1/2"

Cage top or cutout cookies, if desired

5-1/2"

Cage End

5-3/4"

Cage Base

Cage End

5-3/4"

11-1/2"

5-1/2"

5-1/2"

5-1/2"

Index

Index

Index

Index